DATE			

BLACKS IN THE NEW WORLD

August Meier, Series Editor

Before the Ghetto: Black Detroit in the Nineteenth Century   *David M. Katzman*
Black Business in the New South: A Social History of the North Carolina Mutual
    Life Insurance Company   *Walter B. Weare*
The Search for a Black Nationality: Black Colonization and Emigration, 1787–
    1863   *Floyd J. Miller*
Black Americans and the White Man's Burden, 1898–1903   *Willard B. Gate-
    wood, Jr.*
Slavery and the Numbers Game: A Critique of *Time on the Cross*   *Herbert G.
    Gutman*
A Ghetto Takes Shape: Black Cleveland, 1870–1930   *Kenneth L. Kusmer*
Freedmen, Philanthropy, and Fraud: A History of the Freedman's Savings Bank
    Carl R. Osthaus
The Democratic Party and the Negro: Northern and National Politics, 1868–92
    Lawrence Grossman
Black Ohio and the Color Line, 1860–1915   *David A. Gerber*
Along the Color Line: Explorations in the Black Experience   *August Meier and
    Elliott Rudwick*
Black over White: Negro Political Leadership in South Carolina during Recon-
    struction   *Thomas Holt*
Keeping the Faith: A. Philip Randolph, Milton P. Webster, and the Brotherhood
    of Sleeping Car Porters, 1925–37   *William H. Harris*
Abolitionism: The Brazilian Antislavery Struggle   *Joaquim Nabuco, translated
    and edited by Robert Conrad*
Black Georgia in the Progressive Era, 1900–1920   *John Dittmer*
Medicine and Slavery: Health Care of Blacks in Antebellum Virginia   *Todd L.
    Savitt*
King: A Biography   *David Levering Lewis*
The Death and Life of Malcolm X   *Peter Goldman*
Race Relations in the Urban South, 1865–1890   *Howard N. Rabinowitz*
Alley Life in Washington: Family, Community, Religion, and Folklife in the City,
    1850–1970   *James Borchert*
Human Cargoes: The British Slave Trade to Spanish America, 1700–1739
    Colin Palmer

HUMAN CARGOES

Human
Cargoes The British
Slave Trade
to Spanish America,
1700–1739

Colin Palmer

UNIVERSITY OF ILLINOIS PRESS
Urbana   Chicago   London

Cop. 4

Library of Congress Cataloging in Publication Data

Palmer, Colin A., 1942–
  Human cargoes.

  (Blacks in the New World)
  Bibliography: p.
  Includes index.
    1. Slave-trade—Great Britain—History—18th
century.   2. Slave-trade—Africa—History—18th century.   3. Slave-trade—Latin America—History—18th
century.   4. South Sea Company—History—18th century.   I. Title.   II. Series.
HT1161.P34   382'.44'0941   81-3326
ISBN 0-252-00846-4   AACR2

For Glendon, Angie, and Allison

CONTENTS

TABLES

Although an increasing number of scholarly works has appeared within the last decade on the evolution of black life and culture in the Americas, much empirical research still remains to be done. Accordingly, this discussion of the British slave trade to Spanish America seeks to illuminate one of the hitherto neglected aspects of the black diaspora. It also reflects my deeper and continuing interest in the formative years of the African presence in this hemisphere.

I have conceived my study as an exploration of the nature and dimensions of the British slave trade to Spanish America between the years 1700 and 1739. By 1700 Britain had developed a substantial contraband trade with the Spaniards, and during the asiento years (1713—39) her citizens dominated the trade to the Spanish empire. England's share of the Spanish American trade never again reached such proportions as during this period. The major emphasis of the work will therefore be on the asiento years and on the activities of the South Sea Company.

The first part of the book traces the evolution of the British slave trade to Spanish America and its organization and structure on the West African coast during the period. In a few instances, principally in Chapters 1 and 2, I have relied on existing secondary authorities. Chapter 1 provides essential background information by underscoring England's early interest in the Spanish American branch of the trade and demonstrates that the winning of the asiento contract represented the successful culmination of persistent efforts to penetrate and dominate those markets.

Chapter 2 discusses the conduct of the trade on the African coast. It seeks to avoid the artificial distinction that some scholars have made between the ordeal of the slaves on African soil on the one hand and during the Atlantic passage on the other. The slave's experiences cannot be fully understood if historians ignore the continuities in his treatment from the

xiii

moment he became a chattel until his delivery to his new master in the Americas. Underlying this chapter is the further argument that, regardless of the Africans' final destination in the New World, their story was tragically similar. Drawing upon the previously published works of Africanists as well as on fresh evidence, the chapter describes the manner in which the slaves were acquired and the ambivalent nature of Anglo-African relations. In particular, I have explored the uneasy relationship between the African traders and their English counterparts in the service of the Royal African Company, from whom the South Sea Company purchased many slaves. In addition, this chapter shows how African realities were often distorted to suit partisan positions in Britain's domestic politics.

Chapter 3 focuses on the essentially human aspects of the trade by analyzing the incidence of death and disease on the African coast and during the Atlantic passage. I have also devoted some attention to the variegated nature of the Africans' experiences and reactions on board the slavers as they journeyed to one of the Spanish American ports or to Barbados and Jamaica to await transshipment.

The organization and structure of the asiento trade in Spanish America are the primary concern of the remaining two-thirds of the book. These aspects of the slave trade have heretofore remained unstudied, and my interpretations are based on original archival research. Since the majority of slaves who went to Spanish America during the period were transshipped from the West Indian islands, I found it necessary to examine briefly the operations of the South Sea Company in Jamaica and Barbados, the two principal centers of the entrepot trade. Additional chapters contain new data on such topics as the ages, prices, sexual composition, mortality rates, and distribution of the slaves in Spanish America, as well as the profitability of the trade.

The research for this study was facilitated by a fellowship for independent study and research awarded by the National Endowment for the Humanities and by a summer grant from the Research Committee of Oakland University. I am grateful for their support. I also wish to express my appreciation to the staffs of the following institutions for their courtesy and assistance: the British Museum, the Public Record Office (London), the Archivo General de Indias (Seville), the Clements Library (Ann Arbor), and the Kresge Library (Oakland University). Several friends read the manuscript in its earlier stages, either in part or in its entirety, and offered valuable suggestions for improvement. In particular I would like to thank Herbert Klein, Franklin Knight, Joseph Klaits, Joseph Miller, and Monica

Schuler. My deepest debt of gratitude goes to my friend and colleague Gerald Heberle, who read the first draft and made many trenchant criticisms. I found myself adopting his suggestions time and time again. Marian Wilson typed the manuscript with her customary efficiency and her keen eye for stylistic inelegancies and inconsistencies. She helped improve the manuscript in many important ways, and I thank her for her invaluable contributions. Finally, I want to thank my wife, Myrtle, and my children, Glendon, Angie, and Allison, for their interest in the project and their continuing emotional support.

ABBREVIATIONS

AGI   Archivo General de Indias (Seville)
BM   *Additional Manuscripts*, British Museum (London)
CO   *Colonial Office Papers*, Public Record Office (London)
CSP   *Calendar of State Papers, Colonial*, Public Record Office
              (London)
PRO   *Records of the Treasury*, Public Record Office (London)
Shelburne MSS Lord Shelburne Papers, Clements Library (Ann Arbor,
              Mich.)

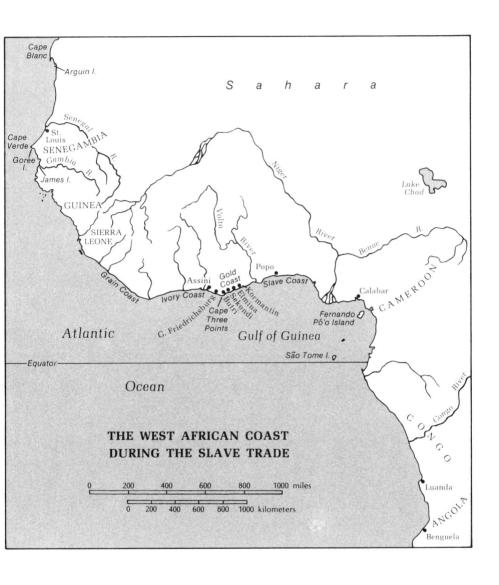

THE WEST AFRICAN COAST
DURING THE SLAVE TRADE

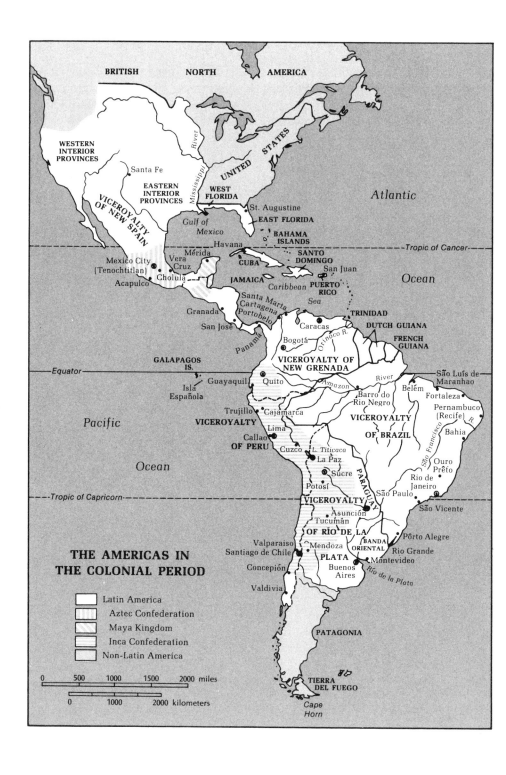

BRITISH   NORTH   AMERICA

WESTERN
INTERIOR
PROVINCES
          Santa Fe
                    EASTERN
                    INTERIOR   WEST
          VICEROYALTY   PROVINCES   FLORIDA   *Atlantic*
          OF NEW SPAIN
                                        St. Augustine
                              Gulf of   EAST FLORIDA
                              Mexico   BAHAMA
                         Havana   ISLANDS   *Tropic of Cancer*
                    Mérida   SANTO
          Mexico City Vera   DOMINGO
          (Tenochtitlan) Cruz   CUBA   San Juan   *Ocean*
          Acapulco Cholula   JAMAICA PUERTO
                                 Caribbean RICO
                              Santa Marta
                              Cartagena   Sea
          Granada   Portobelo   TRINIDAD
                                 Caracas   DUTCH GUIANA
          San José   FRENCH
                         Bogotá Orinoco R. GUIANA
                    Panama
          GALAPAGOS   VICEROYALTY OF
          IS.   NEW GRENADA
Equator
          Isla   Guayaquil Quito   Amazon River   São Luís de
          Española   Barro do Maranhao
                                            Rio Negro Belém
                    Trujillo Cajamarca   VICEROYALTY Fortaleza
Pacific   VICEROYALTY   Lima   Pernambuco
                         Callao   (Recife)
                    OF PERU Cuzco L. Titicaca OF BRAZIL Bahia
                                    La Paz
          Ocean   Sucre   Rio de   Ouro
                         Potosí   Janeiro Prêto
Tropic of Capricorn   VICEROYALTY São Paulo São Vicente
                         Asunción
                         Tucumán
                    OF RÍO DE LA
          Valparaiso Mendoza BANDA Pôrto Alegre
          Santiago de Chile PLATA ORIENTAL Rio Grande
          Concepión   Buenos Montevideo
                           Aires Río de la Plata
          Valdivia

THE AMERICAS IN
THE COLONIAL PERIOD

☐ Latin America
▨ Aztec Confederation
▧ Maya Kingdom
☰ Inca Confederation
☐ Non-Latin America

0   500   1000   1500   2000 miles
0   1000   2000 kilometers

          PATAGONIA

          TIERRA
          DEL FUEGO
          Cape
          Horn

1 The Development of the British Slave Trade to Spanish America

Spain was the first imperial country to introduce African slaves into the Americas. In 1501 the Catholic monarchs Ferdinand and Isabella approved the establishment of slavery in Hispaniola, and the first shipment of blacks arrived on the island the following year. The institution of slavery eventually spread to other areas of the Americas. By the time the various branches of the slave trade ended in the nineteenth century, about 10 million Africans had endured and survived the Atlantic passage. To be sure, the Spaniards were not the only slave traders. The English, French, Portuguese, Dutch, and Danes, among others, participated in the trade. The Portuguese dominated the trade in the formative years, but by the turn of the eighteenth century the English had established their supremacy.

Africans had been enslaved in the Iberian peninsula prior to Columbus's expeditions to the New World, but blacks had comprised only one category in a slave population that included Jews, Arabs, Berbers, and Moors. It must be noted, however, that the Spaniards and the Portuguese became less dependent upon slave labor once their own populations began to increase in the sixteenth century.[1] The situation in Europe was in direct contrast to that in the Americas, where a reduction in the Indian population and the expansion of the colonial economy produced urgent demands for a reliable, servile, and controlled labor force.

The European conquest of the New World led to a drastic decline in the indigenous population. Epidemics of measles, smallpox, and other diseases to which the Indians had no immunity swept the Americas. The population of the Caribbean islands virtually disappeared as a consequence.

In central Mexico the number of Indians fell from about 25 million in 1519 to less than 1.5 million in 1605. Overall, disease and the military effects of the conquest reduced the native population of North and South America from an estimated 80 to 100 million to about 10 million within a century of the first contact with the white man.[2]

This population debacle created serious shortages of labor for the Spaniards. The first conquistadors lacked the numerical strength to exploit fully the resources of the colonies, and many of them also disdained manual labor. Under these circumstances African slaves were imported to fill the void. Recent studies indicate that the Spanish empire received slightly more than 1.5 million slaves between the sixteenth and the nineteenth centuries. Prior to the nineteenth century the majority were sent to Mexico, Peru, Cartagena, and Buenos Aires. After 1800, when sugar became king in Cuba, that island was the most important recipient of slaves in Spanish America. Portuguese Brazil received more slaves than its Spanish-speaking neighbors, having acquired between 3.5 and 5 million Africans during the period in which the trade existed.[3]

Prior to the mid-seventeenth century England's participation in the slave traffic to the New World was both minimal and irregular. Unlike Spain, England did not possess colonies in the Caribbean until the third decade of that century. St. Christopher, the first British colony, was not settled until 1624; Barbados was colonized in 1627; and the larger island of Jamaica was wrested from the Spaniards only in 1655. In addition, during the early years of the seventeenth century the British North American colonies were more dependent upon indentured white labor than upon unfree black workers. As a result of this limited market for slaves, England's interest in the trade was slow to develop.[4]

The development of plantation agriculture in the English possessions, however, created manpower needs which the indentured labor system could not meet. Accordingly, by about 1650 English traders began to manifest a serious and sustained desire to supply their own countrymen and the Spanish empire with all the slaves they needed. This interest gained concrete expression when the Royal Adventurers into Africa, a joint stock company, was chartered in 1660. The Royal Adventurers intended to make a vigorous attempt to supply the Americas with slaves, and in 1663 it even signed a contract to deliver 3,500 of them annually to the Spanish colonies. Unfortunately for the company, however, it soon ran into severe financial difficulties, stemming in part from mismanagement and from seizures by the Dutch of many of its settlements on the African coast. Hence the agreement with the Spaniards remained unfulfilled until the company's demise in 1672.[5]

The Royal African Company, which was chartered in 1672, proved to be more durable than its predecessor and initially more successful. This company survived until 1752, after undergoing several vicissitudes of fortune. The charter granted the company a monopoly to trade, for a period of 1,000 years, between Cape Blanco in the north and the Cape of Good Hope in the south. It was empowered specifically to deal in slaves, gold, and silver and to establish forts and factories at appropriate places on the African coast. As a monopoly company it could seize the ships and effects of interlopers, and a court was created to adjudicate such cases. The governing body of the Royal African Company was an elected court of assistants, which consisted of twenty-four members in addition to a governor, a subgovernor, and a deputy governor.[6]

The years from 1672 to 1698 were crucial in the history of the Royal African Company; in this period it began to establish forts on the coast and to form alliances with several African states for the purpose of protecting and furthering its trade. The company at this time also confronted a concerted effort by private traders to impinge on its monopoly and to provide the West Indian colonists with slaves. These interlopers received a ready acceptance from the planters, who justified their behavior by blaming the company for undersupplying them with African workers.

The Royal African Company, to be sure, fought valiantly to maintain its monopoly. It had to contend with mounting attacks on the principle of monopoly leveled by some members of Parliament, by individual businessmen who were legally excluded from the African trade, and by unhappy West Indian planters. The company eventually compromised. The court of assistants began to issue, in return for a fee, special licenses to some traders that empowered them to sell slaves in the islands, thus tacitly acknowledging that it was unable to execute its monopoly effectively.

The assaults on the company's monopoly and its clear failure to meet the needs of the colonies led Parliament to modify the organization of the African trade in 1698. Private merchants were then authorized to participate freely in the trade for an experimental period of twelve years. In return for this privilege each trader was required to pay the company a fee equivalent to 10 percent of his export cargo's value; consequently these traders became known as "ten percent men." The private traders also had to pay an additional 10 percent duty on the value of all commodities (except redwood, on which the levy was 5 percent) that they imported into

England and which originated in the northern parts of West Africa, specifically between Cape Blanco and Cape Mount. The funds derived from these impositions were to be used for the maintenance of the forts, and the private traders were to have access to these facilities.[7]

The passage of the Ten Percent Act encouraged more private traders to participate in the African slave trade. No longer did they confront the prospect of having their ships and cargoes seized by the Royal African Company. On the other hand, the company found the provisions of the act unacceptable because they severely damaged the monopoly system. Although Parliament was convinced that the national interest and that of the planters and traders could best be served by modifying the monopoly, the company increasingly came to the conclusion that it could not compete effectively with the proliferation of private traders.

The "experimental" years witnessed the gradual ascendancy of the private traders and a steady decline in the fortunes of the Royal African Company. Understandably the company redoubled its efforts to regain the monopoly, while the private traders and their supporters fought to establish completely free trade. Both factions bombarded Parliament with petitions and counterpetitions. In 1707 a commission of enquiry was established to study the African trade and make recommendations on its operation. After prolonged deliberation and careful sifting of the evidence, the commission reported negatively on the monopoly system, and in 1712, when the Ten Percent Act expired, free trade was established. This decision was an additional blow to the company. It was never able to remain a financially viable entity for the remainder of its days. In 1730 the company received a government subsidy of £10,000 per year to help defray the expense of maintaining the forts, but this financial support was insufficient to revive or save the moribund company, which expired in 1752.

The Ten Percent Act had been passed at a time of general expansion in the English trade to Spanish America. As early as 1675 the Royal African Company manifested a guarded interest in that branch of the slave trade. After some study of the prospects for successful trade, however, the court of assistants held that the venture would be worthwhile only if the Spaniards bought their slaves in the English islands and paid the cost of transporting their purchases. Such a conservative decision indicated that the company would participate in the Spanish colonial slave trade only if a profit were virtually certain. Indeed, in 1681 the court of assistants rejected a proposed asiento similar to that signed by the Royal Adventurers in 1663.[8]

The failure to sign a new asiento with the Spaniards did not mean that the English sold them no slaves. On the contrary, the Spaniards came to Jamaica and Barbados to purchase slaves, although the precise number cannot be established. One historian notes that during the 1680s "evidence of a nonstatistical nature" suggests trade on a "considerable scale" between the Spaniards and the English in Jamaica. It is certain that the Spaniards who came to Jamaica paid much higher prices for slaves than did the local residents, a buyers' competition that caused some unhappiness among the planters. In addition, since the Spaniards purchased none but the choicest slaves, the Jamaicans had to take what was left.[9]

In 1689 the company overcame its reluctance to sign an asiento and agreed to deliver 2,000 slaves to the Spaniards in Jamaica within twenty months. As it turned out, this contract was never fulfilled, owing to the immediate outbreak of the Nine Years' War. The company signed no more contracts, although from time to time it looked wistfully at the possibility of developing a vibrant trade with the Spaniards. In 1707, for example, the court of assistants confidently assured the agents at Jamaica that after the War of the Spanish Succession had ended, "we shall endeavour to obtain that contract of supplying the Indies with negroes, and we think we can better perform that agreement than any country or society whatsoever."[10]

That the financially troubled company could have fulfilled the obligations incurred by a new asiento is very doubtful. Under the aegis of the Ten Percent Act, much of the slave trade with the Spaniards fell into the hands of the private traders. Indeed, the private traders claimed in 1708 that in the three previous years they had sold between 6,000 and 7,000 slaves annually to the Spaniards.[11] Three years later some members of the Jamaican Council and Assembly, as well as some merchants, attributed the slave trade to the Spanish colonies chiefly to the efforts of the private traders. They noted that these traders had so well provided the island with slaves that "quantitys of negroes have been yearly exported from hence to ye Spanish West Indies, and there sold for gold and silver."[12]

In the absence of a contract the Anglo-Spanish slave trade was illegal, of course, but it was carried on with the open support of both English and Spanish officials. Both nations profited from this illicit partnership: the Spaniards received the slaves they needed for their households and various economic enterprises; the English had a market for their excess slaves and obtained much-needed bullion. In addition, there was the long-term increase in trade in other commodities that was expected to develop in the wake of the slave trade. The English government consistently supported this illegal commerce during the last third of the seventeenth century and into the early years of the eighteenth. In 1704 the Council of Trade and Plantations informed Queen Anne that two slave ships destined for Africa and Jamaica "might likewise promote the trade with the Spaniards." Four years later the council reminded Governor Crowe of Barbados that he would "do well to give all the encouragement possible to the negroe trade with the Spaniards." Although the slave trade throve with such official support, trade in other commodities was much slower to develop. For example, in 1709 Governor Handasyd of Jamaica reported with some disappointment that "our sloops are all returned from the Spanish coast . . . and have sold little or nothing but negroes." [13]

Throughout the first decade of the eighteenth century the English tried to reduce, if not eliminate entirely, the competition of other European nations in the slave trade to the Spanish empire. English traders and officials were particularly incensed in 1701 when the Spaniards signed an asiento with the French Guinea Company, allowing for the delivery of 4,800 piezas de Indias annually for ten years, beginning in 1702. (A pieza was the standard slave unit.) Once the contract had been signed, Lieutenant Governor George Beckford of Jamaica proposed a scheme to thwart its execution. He suggested that the English keep frigates on the coast of Cartagena and Porto Bello to harass the French; in addition, he thought it might be desirable "to obstruct their trade by our frigotts and all other possible wayes and meanes on the coast of Guinea." Also, the English were to launch a campaign to prevent the Guinea Company from "delivering their negroes at any place or island, particularly the Cape de Verde and adjacent islands, and Hispaniola, or at any Spanish port." He further advised that all English merchants be forbidden to enter into any contractual relationship with the French. Beckford predicted that if all these measures were adopted, "the French will be made incapable of furnishing the quantity [of slaves] contracted for" and "their Asiento must break the first year and then the Spaniards will be glad to take them of the English." [14]

The lieutenant governor's proposals do not appear to have been adopted and executed in any systematic fashion. As attractive as such an undertaking undoubtedly was, it remained far beyond the capacity of the English to accomplish. There were, to be sure, occasional hostile confrontations between the representatives of both nations, but it is doubtful that these were part of a well-planned, coordinated, and financed attempt to cripple the French trade. Actually, the English came off second best in some of their squabbles with the French. In 1704, for example, agent George Jennings of the Royal African Company reported that the *Neptune* "was run ashore on the coast of Guinea after 2 hours engagement with a French man of war of 48 guns." The following year it was revealed that a French "ship of 50 guns had chased several English vessels off the coast but had taken none." Apparently the French on occasion did capture some English vessels. Captain Richard Wallis doubtless expressed the prevailing opinion among English traders when he observed in 1705 that "the Blacks think the French are masters of the world by their taking so many prizes [ships] of other nations and they not see others take any of the French ships." [15]

The eventual failure of the French Guinea Company to meet its contractual obligations had more to do with its own internal difficulties and the problems inherent in the traffic in human merchandise than with English opposition and harassment. In fact, by 1712 the Royal African Company's agent at Jamaica, Lewis Galdy, proposed selling slaves to the French to help them fulfill their contract. Galdy wrote his superiors that the French were short 7,000 slaves in their deliveries to the Spaniards, and he was considering going to Porto Bello and Panama to sell them some of the company's Africans. [16]

Any prospect that the Royal African Company would supply the French with slaves for the Spanish trade was shattered in 1713 with the signing of the Treaty of Utrecht. As part of the price for ending the war, the English wrung an asiento from the reluctant Spanish. The asiento gave the English sole rights to supply the Spanish colonies with slaves for the next thirty years, amounting to 4,800 piezas de Indias annually, an overall total of 144,000 piezas. A duty of 33 1/3 pesos would be paid the Spanish crown on each of the first 4,000 piezas; the remaining 800 would be admitted duty free. In the event that the company delivered more than 4,800 piezas in a year, it would pay a duty of 16 2/3 pesos on each excess pieza. The English could ship slaves to all the colonial ports where royal officers were in residence. The asentista had the power to name judges conservators in each port to adjudicate disputes under the contract. To limit the financial risk of the slave trade, the contract gave the English the right to send one ship each year to one of the three ports where the Spanish traditionally held a commercial fair. This annual ship would be laden with a variety of commodities, and it was expected that the profits from their sale would offset any loss resulting from the trade in slaves. [17]

Many politicians and the negotiators at the peace parley congratulated themselves on having won an enviable prize for their country. On September 11, 1713, the court of assistants of the Royal African Company concluded that the asiento contained "such advantageous terms, as never were before granted to the people who undertook the furnishing negroes to the Spanish West Indies." There was, however, at least one dissenting opinion. George Bubb, the English envoy to Madrid, confessed to Lord Stanhope, the secretary of state, that "I have all along looked upon the Asiento as an affair that we could never be gainers by. . . . I have indeed perused the Asiento treaty and I do think it one of the worst I ever saw and the most effectually calculated for capptiousness and chicane." Events would prove him substantially correct.[18]

Although the asiento had technically been awarded to the English crown, Queen Anne had no intention of being a part of any such commercial operation. On September 7, 1713, the monarch signed over the responsibility for the conduct of the trade to the South Sea Company, which had been chartered in 1711 and granted a monopoly to trade with South America "for ever." The company was governed by an elected court of directors composed of a governor, a subgovernor, a deputy governor, and thirty members.[19]

The company and the Spanish government frequently disagreed over the interpretation of various clauses of the asiento treaty. Prolonged negotiations between England and Spain produced a new convention, signed in 1716, which resolved some of the disputes. The new agreement changed the effective date of the contract from May, 1713, to May, 1714, absolving the South Sea Company from paying duty on the slaves shipped in the year before the peace treaty was formally signed. The convention also stipulated that the company should be notified of the location of the annual fair so that its annual ship could be sent to the proper port.[20]

The convention did not eliminate the deep and abiding distrust which characterized relations between England and Spain, of which the problems arising from the asiento trade were but one reflection. George Bubb observed in 1715 that the Spaniards "are a set of people whose resolutions can never be depended upon, two hours together, nobody can imagine the misfortune it is to have to treat with them."[21] Undoubtedly the Spaniards shared similar sentiments toward "perfide Albion."

The Spaniards, with good reason, accused the English of carrying on a flourishing contraband trade with the colonists. The English never publicly conceded the truth of this allegation, but the issue served further to alienate the two nations. Sporadic warfare also helped ensure the failure of the asiento. Between 1718 and 1721 the slave trade had to be suspended because of the outbreak of war between Spain and England. The trade was reopened in 1722, only to be interrupted a second time when hostilities were renewed in 1727. Trade recommenced after peace was signed in 1729, but the War of Jenkins' Ear, which began in 1739, halted commerce between the belligerents for ten years. The war ended in 1748, but the asiento trade was permanently crippled.

The financial speculation in which the South Sea Company engaged in 1720 also had a negative impact on its commercial operations. When the British government accepted the company's offer to convert part of the national debt into its own stock, this unleashed a speculative boom—the South Sea Bubble—which ultimately ended in a severe crash. The company emerged quite chastened from this disastrous experience. Thereafter, the court of directors de-emphasized trade and other financially risky ventures and kept the bulk of its capital in gilt-edged securities.[22]

Despite the difficulties which the Royal African Company and the South Sea Company faced, the number of Englishmen who participated in the slave trade to the Americas increased throughout the period 1700 to 1739. Most of these traders were based in London, Liverpool, or Bristol. In these three major ports the traders built or contracted for ships, purchased supplies and trade goods, and hired their crews.[23] Each of these tasks required care and expertise, since each was crucial to the success of the venture. The ships must be not only seaworthy but capable of carrying a requisite number of slaves alive and healthy across the ocean; the cargo must include the types of trade goods that were in demand on the African coast; and the crew members must be hardy men likely to survive the rigors of the voyage. Ideally, the crew would have had some prior experience in trading for slaves and in caring for the captives during the long passage to the New World.

The majority of the slave ships sent out by the Royal African and South Sea companies was chartered from private owners. As a matter of fact, the South Sea Company does not appear to have owned any of the ships engaged in the African trade. Typically, the company contracted to pay the shipowner a predetermined freight charge for a given number of slaves. It would hire the crew, provide the trade goods to be exchanged for slaves in Africa, and furnish the provisions for the captives and crew throughout the voyage. In some cases the company made its own arrangements in Africa to obtain slaves; this might involve buying them from the resident factors of the Royal African Company. In other instances the captain of the hired vessel contracted to buy the slaves directly from the African traders on the company's behalf.

Freight charges increased throughout the eighteenth century. In 1715 the Royal African Company paid an average of £5 per head for each slave delivered at Barbados; by 1719 the price had climbed to £7. In general, the freight charge for a slave carried from Africa to Barbados or Jamaica ranged from £5 to £8 during the period 1700 to 1739. For delivery to Buenos Aires, Cartagena, or Porto Bello, the price varied between £6 and £6 10s. during the first few years after the South Sea Company was awarded the asiento. By 1730, however, these charges had increased to between £8 and £10 per slave.[24]

Freight charges varied from ship to ship because the company negotiated separate contracts with each shipowner. The agreements required that the slaves be delivered in a condition "capable of going over the ship's side"—in other words, able to walk. For each slave who died en route to the New World, the company had to pay a dead freight equivalent to 50 percent of the charge for delivering a live slave.[25]

Since every dead slave was a profit loss, the South Sea Company naturally encouraged the captains to take good care of the captives. Experience taught the company that it could not rely on the captain's promise to oversee the welfare of his cargo; a captain would be more apt to follow instructions if he had some financial inducement. For this reason, in 1715 the company decided that each captain of a hired ship would receive four slaves as commission on every 104 that he delivered alive. The court of directors agreed to purchase these slaves from the captain at £20 per head, a not unreasonable sum.[26] The profit motive may have encouraged some captains to take a more benevolent interest in their human cargo, but even this provision probably did not reduce significantly the overall mortality rate of slaves during the Atlantic passage. Slaves fell victim to contagious diseases as often as to poor diet or lack of care.

The captains of these hired vessels were urged to see that the tobacco, beef, and spirits which the company provided for the slaves were actually used by them "and not wasted or embezzled" by crew members, since "waste and embezzlement has sometimes occasioned great mortality amongst the negroes."[27] The instructions given to Captain Nathaniel Smith of the *Essex*, which sailed to Angola in 1723 for a cargo of 400 slaves to be delivered at Buenos Aires, are typical. Captain Smith was required to purchase the slaves and extra provisions with the outward-bound cargo, valued at £3,599 1s. 2d. The slaves were to be between ten and thirty years of age and to be in equal numbers of males and females if possible. Surplus cargo was to be used to purchase gold and ivory, and any unsold portion should be brought back to England unless the company's factors at Buenos Aires needed those commodities for their slaves or for themselves.

Captain Smith was required to keep careful financial records concerning the disposal of the ship's cargo and the purchasing of the slaves, provisions, gold, and ivory. He must account for all his expenditures on the African coast and in Buenos Aires because those charges incurred during the conduct of trade had to be borne by the South Sea Company. Expenses directly related to the ship, such as repairs, were the owner's responsibility. Furthermore, the shipowner was to pay £30 of the total port charges at Buenos Aires. The captain was forbidden to indulge in private trade in Africa "except as shall be allowed by the company." Private trade, if permitted, would be restricted to gold or ivory in order to prevent the captain from competing with the company in the slave trade.

It was the captain's responsibility to ensure that the slaves consumed all the provisions put on board for them. The company valued these provisions at £284 9s. 4d. Captain Smith was advised to buy additional food in Africa if the amount brought from London was insufficient for the slaves. All of the slaves taken on board had to be counted and examined and their age, sex, and physical condition recorded. Each entry in the ledger had to be signed by Captain Smith, the mate, and one other officer.

During the Atlantic passage the slaves were to be mustered every fourteen days and a record kept of the number of dead and the number of survivors, differentiated by age and sex. Deceased slaves could be cast overboard only with the permission of the captain, the first mate, and the surgeon. At the end of the voyage these three men had to produce, under oath, a certificate attesting to the number of slaves that had perished in transit; without such a certificate the captain could not collect his commission or the surgeon his "head money" for each slave under his care.

The captain was further instructed to wash the decks frequently, using vinegar as a disinfectant. The slaves were to be diverted with "music and play" for "the better preservation" of their health. And the crew was forbidden to mix salt water with the slaves' food, since that practice was "very unhealthy for the negroes."

The captain was reminded to store his gunpowder carefully and to make sure that his gunner was a "sober, careful person." He was to be particularly wary of the Portuguese and exercise the utmost caution in dealing with them. If for some reason he had to approach an island under

Portuguese suzerainty, he should take care not to give "any opportunity to make unreasonable demands or detain your ship and ruin your voyage." In addition, the captain should always be on guard against pirates; he was not to leave his ship "and speak to any other without absolute necessity."

Upon arrival in Buenos Aires Captain Smith was required to deliver the slaves to the company's agents and obtain a receipt for them. He was provided with a certificate in Spanish, under the company's seal, attesting that the ship was legitimately freighted according to the terms of the asiento. The certificate was to be produced in the Spanish possessions on demand, "to prevent any seizure or molestation." The captain also carried a copy of the asiento treaty, which he was "to observe and not give any scandal to the Roman Catholic Religion." He also was to carry a copy of the convention of 1716, which explained and amplified some parts of the asiento. For the return passage to London the ship was to be laden with hides and any other merchandise the factors thought appropriate. At the conclusion of the voyage the captain was expected to furnish a written report to the company on the kinds of food he thought most suitable for the slaves and "what method or management may most conduce to their management." The report should also discuss the price of slaves on the coast and what commodities were currently in demand by African traders. Such data, the company hoped, would contribute to the "better regulation" of future cargoes.[28]

The South Sea Company also signed contracts with the Royal African Company for the provision of slaves. In January, 1722, for instance, the Royal African Company agreed to deliver 400 slaves on board the South Sea Company's *Carteret* at Cabinda, at a price of £9 10s. per head. Fifty percent of these slaves were to be males, six-sevenths were to be over sixteen, and the remaining one-seventh boys and girls between ten and fifteen. The slaves were to be loaded within forty-five days after the ship anchored at Cabinda, or sooner if possible. If the ship was not completely loaded within sixty days, the Royal African Company would be liable for £6 10s. per day in demurrage fees. It would have to pay a dead freight charge of £4 10s. for each slave short of the 400.

Under this type of contract the Royal African Company was responsible for the slaves' food while they were on the coast and during the Atlantic passage. The provisions had to be put on board within fifteen days of the ship's arrival. For the *Carteret*'s 400 slaves the company was to provide 320 chests of corn, 200 pounds of malagueta pepper, 16 bushels of salt, 80 gallons of palm oil, and any other necessary supplies. The crew of the *Carteret* could cut wood and draw water at all the areas of the coast controlled by the Royal African Company. Finally, the *Carteret* was to carry from England to Cabinda, freight free, a cargo of goods and stores belonging to the Royal African Company, value not to exceed £2,700.[29]

Chartering ships and sending them on slave-trading voyages was by no means the South Sea Company's only involvement in the trade. It also contracted to buy in New World ports slaves purchased and transported by private shippers. Such contracts would commit the company to buy at a set price all the slaves delivered to the company's agents at a specified port by the private traders' slave ships. The private traders were most anxious to make this kind of contract with the South Sea Company. They submitted tenders to one of the committees of the court of directors which negotiated the contracts and inspected the ships to determine whether they were capable of carrying the requisite number of slaves.[30]

The Royal African Company also sought the same kind of contract with the South Sea Company. In 1721 the Royal African Company contracted to furnish its "sister" company with 3,000 "good and healthy and merchantable negroes, that want neither limb nor eye nor have any dangerous distemper, sore or wound, nor be lame, sick, meagre or refuse." Of these slaves, 2,400 at £22 per head were to come from the Gold Coast, Whydah, and Jakin. The remaining 600 would come from Angola at a price of £18 10s. each. Two-thirds were to be males, and six-sevenths of the total were to be between sixteen and thirty years old. Boys and girls from ten to fifteen years would make up the remaining one-seventh. The two companies agreed that delivery would be made in four equal parts: in May, October, and December, 1721, and February, 1722. Characteristically, the Royal African Company's ambition exceeded its resources and the contract was never fulfilled.[31]

The South Sea Company sent chartered ships regularly to the African coast until 1730, but thereafter, with the greater number of private traders bringing slaves to Jamaica, the company almost gave up the practice. In a newspaper advertisement of 1729 the company announced its decision to buy most of its slaves in Jamaica: "The Court of Directors of the South Sea Company do hereby give notice to all merchants and traders to Guinea and Jamaica that they intend for the future to purchase of them or their agents in that island what negroes they shall want for supply of the Asiento, in expectation of their importing sufficient numbers, and that they shall continue in that method if it be not attended with any unforeseen inconvenience." The court of directors decided to repeat this advertisement annually, since "it will be an inducement to all Guinea traders to import sufficient numbers of negroes into Jamaica." The following year the company sold off all the trading commodities of "Guinea goods" which it had stockpiled for purposes of the African trade. After 1730 the company sent from two to four chartered ships a year to Africa and they always brought slaves to Buenos Aires.[32]

However uncertain the fortunes of the chartered companies or those of the independent businessmen, there is no doubt that their participation in the slave trade was perceived to be in the national interest. Sir Dalby Thomas, the agent general of the Royal African Company at Cape Coast Castle between 1703 and 1711, was convinced that "nothing can make colonies thrive but the cheapness of labour, and this is as certain [that] negroes are the only labourious people to be depended on . . . and as labour is cheape or deare, so is the certain increase or decrease of the wealth and welfare of the colonies."[33] Similar sentiments were voiced in 1717 by the governor of Jamaica: "Planting is the mother of trade and negroes the support of planting."[34] Nine years later a trader of twenty-nine years' experience noted that the slave trade "hath in a very short time risen to the most flourishing state and condition of any other branch of trade now belonging to this nation."[35]

Secure in the knowledge that the national interest and their private needs coincided in the slave trade, an ever larger number of Englishmen began to participate in the traffic in black captives by the early eighteenth century. Not only did these traders supply their own countrymen in the West Indies with slaves but increasingly they began to meet the needs of Spanish America as well. The winning of the coveted asiento opened the Spanish colonies to the South Sea Company and to those independent traders who were bold and aggressive enough to challenge its monopoly. Thus Englishmen joined their traditional enemies, the Spaniards, in an enterprise that they hoped would be mutually beneficial.

NOTES

    1. For a discussion of population trends in early modern Europe, see Marcel R. Reinhard, André Armengaud, and Jacques Dupaquier, *Histoire générale de la population mondiale*, 3d ed. (Paris: Montchrestien, 1968).
    2. Estimates of the Indian population at the time of the European colonization vary. For good discussions of this issue, see Nicolás Sánchez-Albornoz, *The*

Population of Latin America: A History (Berkeley: University of California Press, 1974); Henry F. Dobyns, "Estimating Aboriginal American Population: An Appraisal of Techniques with a New Hemispheric Estimate," *Current Anthropology* 7, no. 4 (Oct., 1966), 395–416; and Woodrow Borah and S. F. Cook, *The Aboriginal Population of Central Mexico on the Eve of the Spanish Conquest*, Ibero-Americana no. 45 (Berkeley: University of California Press, 1963), and *Essays in Population History* (Berkeley: University of California Press, 1971).

3. Philip D. Curtin has estimated that about 1,552,000 slaves went to Spanish America during the entire period of the slave trade. See *The Atlantic Slave Trade: A Census* (Madison: University of Wisconsin Press, 1969), p. 46. Curtin's figures may be revised by future research.

4. The experiences of the English in the early years of settlement in the West Indies are recounted in Richard S. Dunn, *Sugar and Slaves: The Rise of the Planter Class in the English West Indies, 1624–1713* (Chapel Hill: University of North Carolina Press, 1972).

5. The Royal Adventurers was reorganized and granted a new charter in 1663. Prior to 1660 the English established two joint stock companies for the purpose of obtaining a share of the African commerce. Known as the Senegal Adventurers, the first company was chartered in 1588 to conduct trade between Senegal and Gambia for ten years. There is no evidence that this company engaged in the slave trade. The second company, the Governor and Company of Adventurers of London trading to Gynney and Bynney (Guinea and Benin), was formed in 1618. Again, it is not certain if this company engaged in the slave trade. See K. G. Davies, *The Royal African Company* (1957; reprinted, New York: Atheneum Press, 1970), pp. 38–44; George F. Zook, *The Company of Royal Adventurers Trading into Africa* (Lancaster, Pa.: New Era Printing Co., 1919), pp. 1–7.

6. Davies, *Royal African Company*, pp. 97–99.

7. Ibid., pp. 134–35.

8. Ibid., p. 328.

9. Ibid., pp. 328–35. See also Leslie Imre Rudnyanszky, "The Caribbean Slave Trade: Jamaica and Barbados, 1680–1770" (Ph.D. thesis, Notre Dame University, 1973); F. J. Osborne, "James Castillo, Asiento Agent," *Jamaica Historical Review* 8 (1971), 9–18.

10. Great Britain, Public Record Office, *Records of the Treasury*, no. 70, vol. 58, p. 139 (hereafter cited as PRO, T70).

11. PRO, T70/175, p. 27.

12. Great Britain, Public Record Office, *Calendar of State Papers, Colonial*, no. 582 (1710–11), p. 336 (hereafter cited as CSP).

13. PRO, T70/175, p. 221; CSP, no. 156 (1704–5), p. 64; no. 210 (1708–9), p. 155; no. 542 (1709), p. 320.

14. CSP, no. 489 (1702), pp. 323–24.

15. PRO, T70/14, pp. 70, 76, 109.

16. PRO, T70/8, p. 63.

17. Great Britain, House of Lords Record Office, *Main Papers, Parchment Collection*, Box 157.

18. London, British Museum, *Additional Manuscripts*, vol. 2172, p. 185 (hereafter cited as BM); 25562, p. 6; 2171.

19. See BM, 25494 for the company's charter.

20. BM, 2172, p. 185.

21. BM, 2170.

22. For discussion of the South Sea Bubble, see John G. Sperling, *The South Sea Company: An Historical Essay and Bibliographical Finding List* (Cambridge, Mass.: Harvard University Press, 1962), pp. 25–38.

23. In 1721, for example, Bristol had sixty-three ships in the trade capable of carrying 16,950 slaves annually. Liverpool had twenty-one ships in 1726 with a capacity of 5,200 slaves, while London boasted eighty-seven slave ships capable of accommodating 26,440 slaves. See PRO, T70/172, pp. 24, 29–33; T70/175, p. 117; Great Britain, Public Record Office, *Colonial Office Papers*, vol. 137, no. 12, 311 (hereafter cited as CO).

24. BM, 25575, pp. 26–28; 22508, p. 65.

25. BM, 25575, pp. 26–28.

26. BM, 25575, p. 25.

27. See BM, 25567 passim, for examples of contracts.

28. See BM, 25567, for the text of the contract.

29. The South Sea Company signed a few other contracts with the Royal African Company. The general terms of these contracts were similar to the one discussed, except that the quantities of provisions and the value of the freight-free cargoes varied in accordance with the number of slaves to be put on board. On May 16, 1723, for example, the Royal African Company contracted to supply the *Sea Horse* with 325 slaves. According to the agreement, the ship would transport £2,400 worth of commodities freight free for the company, and the company's agents in Africa would provide 260 chests of corn, 163 pounds of malagueta pepper, 13 bushels of salt, and 65 gallons of palm oil for the slaves. See BM, 25575, pp. 89–92, 95–98. Available data suggest that between Oct. 17, 1722, and Oct. 25, 1723, the South Sea Company purchased 2,901 slaves from the Royal African Company on the African coast. See PRO, T70/1186, p. 84.

30. In 1732 the *Rudge* was contracted to deliver 450 slaves from Angola to Buenos Aires at £20 per head; all slaves in excess of this total would be sold at £17 10s. each. Two years later the owners of the *Hiscox* and the *Anne* agreed to deliver 380 and 320 slaves respectively at Buenos Aires for £20 per head. See BM, 25504, p. 205; 25507, pp. 106, 172; 25509, pp. 159, 165.

31. BM, 25575, pp. 74–77.

32. BM, 25503, p. 293; 25504, p. 213.

33. PRO, T70/175, p. 45.

34. CO, vol. 137, no. 12, 311. See also PRO, T70/175, pp. 44, 182, for similar opinions.

35. CO, vol. 388, no. 25, 295–96.

2 The Structure of the Trade in Africa

The British slave trader in Africa was at once a businessman, a diplomat, and a soldier. To wring the maximum profit from trade, he had to pick his way through the complexities of African politics, forestall his European rivals, and overmatch his own country's traders in astuteness and tenacity. On any given day he might have to drive a hard bargain, fight a battle, or conduct a delicate negotiation. The vast cultural differences between the black trader and his white counterpart also complicated the trading process. These difficulties notwithstanding, the Englishman and the African were locked together, albeit uneasily, through mutual trading interests. Each wanted what the other had to offer, and therefore each was willing to suffer the other's seemingly peculiar manners.

Clearly, neither the Englishmen nor the Africans accepted or completely trusted each other. In fact, Englishmen of the eighteenth century considered themselves superior to the black Africans and were likely to think the worst of them. There was nothing new about that. It is now generally recognized that the English held negative assumptions about blacks as early as the sixteenth century, the period of first contact between the two peoples. The color black was imbued with all sorts of negative connotations. In addition, Englishmen found African customs and beliefs strange and bewildering.[1] White visitors to the black continent seldom developed an understanding of or appreciation for the ways of their hosts. The reports of the Royal African Company's agents on the coast during the eighteenth century often reflected their conscious and unconscious assumption of superiority. Many of the traders' observations were deliberate distortions of the African reality and were frequently designed to influence English opinion for political purposes.

Immediately after the Ten Percent Act was passed in 1698, for example, the Royal African Company mounted an energetic campaign to persuade Parliament and the public that the act was a mistake and was harmful to trade. The company portrayed the Africans as so unruly, dishonest, and barbaric that trade could be conducted only from heavily fortified centers. Since the private traders could never build and maintain forts, their participation would reduce the slave trade and impoverish the West Indian plantations. In 1709, as part of the company's propaganda, Sir Dalby Thomas and two of his associates at Cape Coast Castle wrote an article entitled "A true and impartial account of what we by long experience do know [and] to the best of our observations do believe most proper for the well carrying on of this trade." This tendentious document was submitted to Parliament in support of a petition for exclusive trading rights on the coast.

Sir Dalby, probably the sole author, painted a picture of unrelieved barbarism and lawlessness in Africa:

> The natives here has neither religion nor law binding them to humanity, good behaviour or honesty. They frequently for their grandeur sacrifice an innocent man, that is, a person they have no crime to charge with; and to train their children up to cruelty they give them knives to cut and slash the person that is to be killed, neither have they any knowledge of liberty and property. . . . Besides the blacks are naturally such rogues and bred up with such roguish principles that what they can get by force or deceit and can defend themselves from those they robb, they reckon it as honestly their own, as if they paid for it.[2]

Thomas was repeating an already established company line. As early as 1697 it had held that the Africans "are a people so treacherous and barbarous that no treaties of peace will oblige them and they watch all opportunities to kill and steal."[3] The court of assistants charged in 1708 that Africans "are illiterate people and have not (or are govern'd by) any religion, lawes or courts of justice, or any civiliz'd rules of discipline."[4] Thomas's 1709 article gave the sanction of "experts" to such views, and the court of assistants confidently informed Parliament that "the natives of Africa are a barbarous and uncivilized people and the methods of trading with them are altogether different from those practiced between European and other civilized nations."[5] Dr. James Houstoun, a surgeon working for the company on the coast, added his authority to this negative version in 1725: "[The Africans'] natural temper is barbarously cruel, selfish, and deceitful, and their government equally barbarous and uncivil; and consequently, the men of greatest eminency amongst them, are those that are most capable of being the greatest rogues; vice being left without any check on it, becomes a virtue. As for their customs, they exactly resemble their fellow creatures and natives, the monkeys."[6]

The accumulated observations made by the traders provided a consistent pattern of denigration in what Englishmen read about Africans in the early eighteenth century. Toward the end of the century, however, when the slave trade was under attack by the abolitionists, some traders found it politic to paint a decidedly more positive picture of the African and his customs. If they could show that the slave traffic had no deleterious effect on the Africans and their societies, then the arguments used against the trade would carry little weight. The reports now sought to demonstrate that the blacks were "civilized," that trade followed a rational pattern, and that, far from being lawless and barbarous, African societies were governed by stable and intelligent rulers.

Dalby Thomas had written in 1709, "Nothing is commoner from the greatest to the least of them than to steal one another and run them on shipboard to sell."[7] But in the late eighteenth century some traders who testified before the various official enquiries into the trade emphatically denied that Africans kidnapped other Africans for the slave market. These "eyewitnesses" described sophisticated societies that consigned only criminals and conquered enemies to slavery. And even criminals, they asserted, were not enslaved until their guilt had been proven by an impartial trial.[8]

Neither Sir Dalby's description in 1709 nor the testimony of these traders was intended to present the truth, but each had some effect in shaping British opinion. Each was meant to influence the British public at different times and for different reasons. Clearly, many of the enduring myths about Africa and Africans were created and perpetuated to serve partisan positions in England's domestic politics.

Regardless of cultural prejudice, there was potentially too much money to be made in the trade for either side to indulge its dislikes too freely. The English knew that good relations with the African peoples were essential for successful business operations. The court of assistants of the Royal African Company instructed its new employees to treat the Africans "gently and courteously" and to "keep friendly correspondence with the kings, cabashiers [caboceers] and other great men." Agents should "ingratiate" themselves with local officials and traders so that "they may become assured that the company's design is nothing but trade." The company hoped

that good will and a friendly spirit not only would bring the desired financial rewards from increased trade but would convince the blacks that the
English deserved preferment over their European competitors.[9]

In order to foster, develop, and protect their trade, the chartered companies established a series of settlements or trading posts along the coast.
The Portuguese at Elmina had begun to construct fortified settlements as
early as 1492. In time, many other European nations that engaged in the
African trade adopted the same method.[10] The Royal African Company
was strongly committed to constructing and maintaining settlements, but
the South Sea Company and the private traders never had the inclination
or the financial resources to carry out such an undertaking. These enclaves
ranged in importance and ostentation from well-fortified enclosures consisting of several buildings to small factories with no more than one or two
crude structures. By and large, factories were temporary and could be
abandoned at no great loss if and when trade fell off. The forts were a
more permanent investment than the factories and were constructed only
at places with a potential for abundant and sustained trade.[11]

The Royal African Company's principal settlement was Cape Coast
Castle, situated in Fetu on the Gold Coast. It was fortified with outworks,
platforms, and bastions and was the chief repository of goods for the other
forts and factories. The two small forts of Queen Anne's Point and Fort
Royal were adjacent to the castle. Other company forts on the Gold Coast
included Sekondi, Accra, Dixcove, Komenda, Winneba, and Anomabo. In
the Senegambia the Royal African Company constructed James Island and
York Island forts, and it built Bence Island fort in Sierra Leone. William's
Fort was located at Whydah on the Slave Coast.[12]

Although the forts constituted an effective means of conducting trade
on the coast, it must be recognized that ultimately the supply of slaves was
in large measure a reflection of the political fragmentation in Africa during the period of this study and in other years. West Africa, the principal
arena of the trade during the early decades of the eighteenth century, consisted of numerous competing societies of varying sizes and degrees of
power and influence. The inhabitants of the respective political entities invariably shared a common descent. These lineage ties served on the one
hand to unite the residents of each society, but on the other they ensured
that outsiders would be viewed as "nonpersons" who could be acquired,
enslaved, or sold without undue moral compunction.[13]

Africans acquired their slaves in a variety of ways. Many were captives taken in war, others were kidnapped, and some were obtained by

rulers as tribute payments. Orphans could be purchased as slaves. Convicted criminals might be sold into slavery. During times of economic distress slaves could be obtained as barter. The Atlantic trade did not alter these basic ways in which slaves were traditionally procured. It is becoming increasingly clear, however, that the slaves who were sold to the Europeans were not drawn in any significant sense from those who had become integral parts of their host society. These "internal slaves" were liable to be sold only under the most unusual circumstances. Francis Moore, a British slave trader, reported that in the Gambia a "slave" could not be sold for committing a crime unless his peers approved. Even some of the traders who testified during the official enquiries into the slave trade admitted that "internal slaves" were not normally offered for sale.[14]

It seems reasonable to conclude that the Africans who were sold to the English as slaves were primarily recently acquired war captives, victims of abduction, or condemned criminals. What proportion of the whole each category comprised cannot be precisely determined, yet there is some evidence that a majority of these slaves had been the casualties of war. "Most of the slaves that are offered to us," wrote the Dutch slave trader William Bosman in the early eighteenth century, "are prisoners of War which are sold by the victors as their booty." Bosman was referring to slaves purchased at Whydah, but his dictum seems equally applicable to the rest of the coast.[15]

Throughout the early eighteenth century wars occurred frequently in the areas of West Africa where the slave trade was particularly extensive. Political fragmentation and intersocietal rivalries and jealousies created all the usual occasions for warfare: revenge, trade rights, succession disputes, territorial expansion, and so on. It is tempting to conclude that the European presence and the slave trade triggered many of these wars. Perhaps, but the evidence presently available is fragmentary, uncertain, and ambiguous. An uncritical reliance on European sources may lead to an exaggerated emphasis on the white foreigners' role in African statecraft and to an underestimation of the Africans' independence in managing their own destinies.

It can be more accurately maintained that the overseas slave trade supplemented but did not replace the essentially local reasons for warfare in West Africa. A considerable proportion of the conflicts during the years 1700–1739 resulted from programs of territorial expansion undertaken by various societies.[16] The slave trade certainly exacerbated intersocietal relations; minor disputes now often led to war because captives could be profitably sold to the Europeans. The English and other traders provided the firearms and powder that may have encouraged aggression by the better armed societies. In 1715, for example, a Royal African Company agent at Komenda reported a brisk market for guns and gunpowder because "the traders are going to war with a country behind their own."[17]

Sometimes, to be sure, African societies did engage in war with the principal objective of obtaining captives for the slave market. The Royal African Company records, for example, mention one war in 1711 that was waged primarily to obtain slaves. The factors reported that the Fante had attacked the Fetu "and took most of the women and children but the men escaped." The battle had been triggered by the "10 per cent men's great demand for slaves" and by the jealous rage of the Fante over the close alliance between the English and the Fetu.[18]

English slave traders at times reacted gleefully when wars broke out between Africans, since more captives would be available for purchase. Josiah Pearson of the Royal African Company wrote excitedly from Anomabo in 1706 that the company's employees were "in daily expectation of the Arcanians coming to fight the Cabes-terra People which if they beat there will be a glorious trade both for slaves and gold." To a description of the political dissension between the various societies adjacent to Cape Coast in 1712, the agent added, "The battle is expected shortly, after which 'tis hoped the trade will flourish."[19] The company was often ambivalent about these conflicts, for a war that invigorated the slave trade could badly disrupt the trade in gold and ivory. Worse, war could bring all trade to a standstill.

There is an important distinction, to be sure, between officially declared wars and abduction missions. Like wars, abductions were facilitated by internal divisions as well as by intersocietal disputes. While it is not possible to indicate how many people fell victim to kidnappers, there is little doubt that the practice was widespread.

Opportunities for Englishmen to abduct Africans directly were limited to the general restriction of the white men's activities to their coastal settlements, to the principal rivers, or, in the case of many private traders, to their ships.[20] Most white traders were rightly afraid to venture into the unknown and mysterious interior, while African middlemen protected their lucrative trade by preventing the outsiders from establishing direct contact with the suppliers of slaves. On occasion, however, a ship's captain would enslave an African trader who came on board. Trader William Snelgrave, for example, observed that on the Windward Coast French and

English traders abducted black traders "under some slight pretence of having received an injury from them." [21]

There are also indications that Englishmen made kidnapping raids on African land. William Bosman reported in 1702 that the people at Cape Mesurado told him that "the English had been there with two large Vessels, and had Ravaged the Country, destroyed all their Canoa's, Plundred their Houses, and carried off some of their People for Slaves." [22] Such a brazen raid by Englishmen acting alone was evidently quite unusual; by the eighteenth century onshore kidnapping with the assistance of blacks was probably more common. The Royal African Company does not seem to have encouraged such activities, but at least a few of its agents engaged in them anyway. [23]

The Africans often reacted violently against the carrying off of their relatives and friends by committing depredations against any vulnerable and available Englishmen. Thus private traders who could hit and run left the Royal African Company's permanent residents to bear the responsibility. For example, when the captains of the *New London* and the *Empress* seized sixteen Africans at York Island in 1698 and "put them in irons with an intent to carry them to the West Indies," several hundred irate residents of the area attacked the factory of the Royal African Company. In 1702 four captains, apparently acting in concert, abducted twenty-four Africans and their trading goods at Komenda, where the ships were anchored. Hoping to placate the enraged Africans on shore, the company's agents redeemed some of the victims at the price of three slaves for every abducted black. These efforts were not enough; a few days later "great quantities" of Africans, under the pretext of trading, invaded the newly arrived *Dolphin*, ransacked its cargo, and ran it aground. The sloop broke up and the captain and most of the crew were captured but later released. Captain Bernard Ladman, evidently a witness to the affair, was convinced that unless the English ceased kidnapping Africans, "our English colonies will be of no use to us for the negroes study revenge and are resolved to seize upon what they can." [24]

It may be argued that Africans were abducted by other Africans—particularly those from neighboring societies—far oftener than by Europeans. Many times the African who abducted someone from a rival society regarded himself as merely waging war by another means. Such an act was risky, however, for if discovered it could exacerbate the differences between the two societies and foment open war. In one report to his superiors Sir Dalby Thomas noted that the people on the coast preferred to abduct those "in the bush." As Thomas put it, the coastal peoples "very often panyar [abduct] the Bush people a coming down to buy fish and sells them on board ship and it's no fault unless found out." [25]

To be sure, there were occasions when individuals kidnapped their unsuspecting countrymen and sold them, but such acts appear to have been fairly rare. "Not a few in our country fondly imagine that parents here sell their children, men their wives and one brother the other," wrote William Bosman about Whydah and, by implication, all the coast during the eighteenth century. "But," he added, "those who think so deceive themselves." An English trader also spoke with considerable truth in 1726: "'Tis well known that nine parts in ten of the slaves are of other countrys." [26]

The tales of African kings burning and devastating entire villages of their own subjects and selling the inhabitants to the Europeans are grossly exaggerated. Had such atrocities been common, white traders and visitors on the coast would not have failed to describe them in graphic detail. In fact, lurid stories of this kind are relatively scarce, at least for the years covered by this study. Francis Moore mentioned, in the 1730s, a king of Saalum in the Gambia who habitually attacked his own villages at night, set fire to the houses, and seized the escaping residents for the slave market. Rulers who indulged in this kind of infamy probably lost more than they gained. Indeed, as Moore pointed out, the power of Fooni and Cumbo was declining because their kings had sold "infinite numbers of their subjects" into slavery. [27]

The third category of slaves consisted of those persons who lost their freedom as a result of judicial action. Individuals convicted of theft, murder, and adultery were liable to be sold into slavery. Debtors could be sold to redeem their debts, as could persons who failed to pay fines imposed by a court. Snelgrave said that indigent families who were unable to care for their children sold them into slavery, but it seems likely that these children were sold to local Africans so that the parents might have a chance to redeem them. [28]

It appears to be true, as Moore alleged, that in order to raise revenue it became the practice in some societies to sell into slavery individuals convicted of the most innocuous offenses. "Since this slave trade has been us'd, all punishments are chang'd into slavery," Moore wrote, with some exaggeration. "Not only murder, theft, adultery are punish'd by selling the criminal for a slave, but every trifling crime is punish'd in the same manner." [29] There is no credible evidence, however, that a significant proportion of the slaves shipped to the Americas was criminal. Had the enslavement of criminals been a major source of slaves, it seems certain that an experienced trader like Dalby Thomas would have mentioned it. The fact that he did not suggests that the practice was not widespread. It seems certain that when the slavers' apologists in the late eighteenth century asserted that the majority of African slaves were convicted criminals, they were grossly misstating the facts.[30]

Whatever the mode by which slaves were obtained for the markets of the Americas, the supply was conditioned primarily by factors peculiar to each region at a particular time. Much depended on the political climate—whether the African societies were at war or at peace. The competition between the European traders for the available slaves, and the high prices offered for them, probably had a positive impact on supply in some societies, but the degree is difficult to measure.[31]

Available data suggest that African traders were least likely to sell their slaves during planting and harvesting periods. The captives were evidently being employed in agrarian tasks and were only parted with when their labor was no longer required. This was the case during the eighteenth century in Gajaaga, Senegambia, where slave owners used their slaves to plant millet prior to selling them to the French. There is also some indication that African traders were reluctant to sell female slaves to the Europeans. Women were highly prized, partly because they performed agricultural labor in the local societies. Women of childbearing age were also at a premium because their children contributed to the greatly desired population increase. It is not surprising, therefore, that women commanded double the price of men in the domestic slave markets of the Senegambia in the last decades of the seventeenth century.[32] Clearly, it cannot be confidently asserted that African suppliers responded uniformly and consistently to the manpower requirements of the Europeans and that a simple demand-and-supply relationship existed. Further research will surely provide more information on the nature of the control that the Africans exercised over the timing, the supply, and the volume of the trade. Ultimately, we will also have a deeper understanding of the unique characteristics of each trading region and of changes in the recruitment of the slaves over time.

Slaves who landed in Spanish America during the first four decades of the eighteenth century were taken principally from the coastal area of West and Central Africa, an area bounded roughly by the Senegal River and Angola and probably extending a few hundred miles into the interior. Senegambia, the northernmost section, comprised that area between the

Senegal and Gambia rivers. The adjacent region, Sierra Leone, had different boundaries from the present-day country of the same name. In the eighteenth century Sierra Leone included roughly the area bounded by the Casamance River and Cape Mount. Among the most important peoples inhabiting the Senegambia and Sierra Leone during the period of this study were the Fulbe, the Wolof, the Serer, and the Malinke.

Sierra Leone's neighbor, the Windward Coast, lying between Cape Mount and Assini, was roughly equivalent to present-day Liberia and the Ivory Coast. This area, although encompassing many societies, was not a major center of the English slave trade during the early eighteenth century. The Royal African Company built no forts there, although its ships and those of the private traders did not altogether avoid that part of the coast. The Windward Coast was particularly noteworthy for its malagueta pepper and, to a lesser extent, ivory.

Farther to the east lay the Gold Coast, the principal slave-trading area in West Africa at that time. This coastal zone, equivalent to contemporary Ghana, was bounded by Assini on the west and the Volta River on the east. It was the homeland of such peoples as the Akan, the Guan, and the Ga-Adangbe. There were a number of important societies in the Gold Coast by the eighteenth century; among these were Fetu, Asebu, Fante, Agona, Accra, Ante, and Eguafo. Inland from these essentially coastal territories were such kingdoms as Akwamu, Great Inkassa, Akanny, Denkyera, Akyem, Ashanti, and Kabestera. The Gold Coast was the scene of the most intense competition between the European nations for supremacy in the slave trade; consequently this region was saturated with foreign forts.

The Slave Coast, the fifth principal trade area, comprised the modern nations of Dahomey and Togo. The states of Ardra and Whydah were two of the most prominent slave suppliers in this region during the early eighteenth century. The Bight of Biafra, an area bounded roughly by the Benin River to the west and Cape Lopez to the south, formed the sixth area from which the English obtained slaves. This trading zone, probably because it was infested with mosquitoes and was generally unhealthy for whites, had no Royal African Company forts. The Ibo, who came from this general region, were considered tractable and hence were highly sought after by some of the slaveholders in the Americas. The seventh area from which the English obtained slaves was Angola, at the time a large area of no precise boundaries lying both north and south of the Congo River. An eighth source of a few slaves was the island of Madagascar off the coast of southeastern Africa.[33]

An analysis of 134 slave ships that the South Sea Company hired and apparently dispatched to Africa between 1713 and 1736 reveals that forty-four (32.8 percent) of them went to Angola. Of the remainder, thirty-one (23 percent) left for the Gold Coast and twenty-five (18.7 percent) for the Slave Coast. Only eleven ships (8 percent) sailed for the Senegambia. Several of the ships intended to make more than one stop on the coast (see Table 1); the company evidently felt that a ship calling at several places stood a better chance of filling its quota.[34]

A wide assortment of goods was required for the slave trade: several types of guns, gunpowder, British woolen and textile products, East Indian textiles, and miscellaneous items such as mirrors, alcohol, knives, iron bars, pipes, tobacco, and beads.[35] An ill-chosen assortment for a particular area resulted in a poor market and even produced dissension between the traders and the Africans. In 1715 the black traders at York Island fort at the River Sherbro raged at agent John Ball when he offered them trade goods they despised, particularly some small brass kettles which, the agent lamented, "only breed a disturbance, the natives threatening to throw them in our people's faces." To minimize this kind of angry protest, the Royal African Company's agents submitted periodic reports on the types of goods demanded by their customers. The South Sea Company also required its captains to report on the current state of the African market.[36]

By the eighteenth century a monetary standard had developed in most regions where the slave trade existed. A system of gold weights was used to determine value on the Gold Coast, cowrie shells formed the monetary unit on the Slave Coast, iron bars in the Senegambia, and palm cloth on the Loango Coast. Under normal circumstances business was not conducted on the basis of a unit-for-unit equivalence, that is, one iron bar or one cowrie shell or one ounce of gold being exchanged for one slave. Rather, the regular practice was to use a "commodity currency," whereby an assortment of one set of goods would be exchanged for an assortment of another. In other words, a number of slaves deemed to have a value of, say, 200 iron bars would be exchanged for an assortment of European goods of equivalent value. The process was much more complex than a system of simple barter, since barter usually involved the exchange of one item for another.[37]

Although the traders carefully calculated the volume of merchandise they would need to purchase a given number of slaves, prices were generally too uncertain to allow much precision. With good luck a trader would

TABLE 1. Destination of 134 South Sea Company Slave Ships, 1714–38

Destination	Number of Ships	Percentage
Angola	44	32.8
Gold Coast	31	23.1
Slave Coast	25	18.7
The Senegambia	11	8.2
Windward Coast	1	0.7
Madagascar	6	4.5
Slave and Gold coasts	1	0.7
Slave, Gold, and Windward coasts	1	0.7
Windward and Gold coasts	4	3.0
Gold Coast and the Senegambia	1	0.7
Unknown	9	6.7
Total	134	100.0

SOURCE: BM, 25494-584. Percentages have been rounded.

have goods left over which could be exchanged for gold, ivory, or some other commodity. To be on the safe side, the South Sea Company often shipped cargoes in excess of the estimated amount necessary to purchase the intended quantity of slaves. Records of twenty ships that the South Sea Company sent to Africa between 1723 and 1726 permit us to study this aspect of the trade.

According to the company, the cargo for twelve of these twenty ships was more than adequate to purchase the expected number of slaves. The cargo on the remaining eight ships was held to be sufficient to cover the cost of their slaves and perhaps to buy additional provisions. Of the eight ships whose cargo was merely adequate, seven went to Angola and the eighth to Madagascar. An analysis of the instructions given to the captain and of the slave capacity for the eighth ship shows that the company expected to pay £2 8s. per slave at Madagascar in London prices of cargo, or £4 16s. if calculated on the basis of the projected selling price of those goods in Africa.[38] This rather low price reflected the fact that Madagascar, by virtue of its distance from the Americas, was not a principal slave-trading area. In the absence of any real competition the company expected to buy cheaply.

The other ships' records show that the South Sea Company anticipated paying an average of about £10 6s. in London prices, or about

£20 12s. in African prices, for the slaves it purchased in Angola. This projected cost was well in excess of what most private traders and the Royal African Company could afford to pay. These estimates may substantiate the oft-repeated charge that the South Sea Company was extravagant in the prices it paid for slaves, a practice that its detractors claimed had an inflationary effect on the coast. Critics of the company noted that it paid more for slaves simply because it could resell them in Spanish America at much higher prices than those which prevailed in the English colonies. The company retorted—correctly—that the Spaniards purchased only the best slaves, which were more expensive on the coast. Table 2 shows the values of each cargo, the number of slaves the cargo was intended to purchase, and the projected average cost of each slave.

Although most commercial transactions between the Africans and the English were conducted on a "cash" basis, sometimes credit had to be advanced to one party or the other. The African trader who obtained goods on credit promised to repay the debt in such commodities as slaves, gold, or ivory. English debtors usually gave a promissory note to acknowledge indebtedness. Some of the debts contracted by white traders were for a short term. William Snelgrave, for example, spoke of owing the traders at Whydah "goods on my notes for ten days together, because the badness of the sea prevented our landing them." The Dahomeans did not take kindly to selling slaves on credit, however; they told Snelgrave they "did not like a bit of paper for their slaves, because the writing might vanish from it, or else the notes might be lost, and then they should lose their payment."[39] The Africans evidently had good reasons for concern, since European traders could owe them huge sums of money. During 1737, 1739, and 1741, for example, the Royal African Company's credits in the Gambia amounted to about twice its debts.[40]

Presents given to the Africans formed a useful emollient in maintaining cooperative trading relations. "Treating of traders is no small article and must be done if the trade is to be carried on to its utmost," Sir Dalby Thomas wrote in 1709. The agents at Cape Coast Castle noted that there was a quid pro quo in presenting gifts: "Those who make the most acceptable presents has the most friendship from them, and tho' the great men are seldom traders, yet it is very much in their power to command and influence the traders to the place they recommend to them."[41]

The bestowal of gifts in many instances created a favorable disposition toward the English, but a durable and successful trading relationship required a solid foundation of mutual profit. The chartered companies and

TABLE 2. Value of Cargo and Projected Cost of Slaves, 1723–26

Year	Ship	Destination	Number of Slaves Intended	Value of Cargo (£ s. d.)	Projected Cost of Slaves	
					Cost of Cargo in England (£ s. d.)	Selling Price in Africa (£ s. d.)
1723	*Essex*	Angola	400	3,599 1. 2.	9 0. 0.	18 0. 0.
1723	*Syrria*	Angola	500	4,623 10. 0.	9 5. 0.	18 10. 0.
1723	*Levantine*	Angola	380	3,399 3. 8.	9 0. 0.	18 0. 0.
1724	*Bonita*	Angola	520	5,659 17. 6	10 17. 0.	21 14. 0.
1724	*Boothe*	Angola	434	4,892 4. 8.	11 5. 0.	22 10. 0.
1725	*Duke of Cambridge*	Angola	480	5,214 13. 9.	10 17. 0.	21 14. 0.
1725	*King William*	Angola	500	5,868 13. 4.	11 14. 0.	22 8. 0.
1726	*Sea Horse*	Madagascar	412	991 2. 5.	2 8. 0.	4 16. 0.

SOURCE: BM, 25567.

the private traders had to supply what the Africans needed and wanted in return for their slaves, gold, and ivory. One agent summarized the situation very well: "Your presents and power . . . may subject these waterside people to your interest but if your warehouses are not kept constantly supplied with all sorts of goods, your presents and power is to no consequence."[42]

Political alliances between the English and the leaders of the African societies were a more concrete and effective way of ensuring regular supplies of slaves and other commodities.[43] Not very surprisingly, the alliances were often unreliable, since both the English and the Africans based their conduct on a sophisticated evaluation of their own interests. These alliances not infrequently involved the company in African politics and entangled it in an endless series of local disputes and wars. Agent John Snow was of the opinion that "the concerning ourselves in the succession of their kings" was one reason for the Royal African Company's "misfortune."[44]

English traders, on occasion, interfered directly in the domestic affairs of the Africans. Agents might, for example, usurp the right of African authorities to try and punish their own citizens for crimes. Sir Dalby Thomas reported in 1709 that he had made "some of the Fettuers suffer" as a result of their "imposing on an Ashanti trader." Agent Cruischank went even further at Winneba in 1730. When some of the residents refused Cruischank's request for a number of their captives, he retaliated by seizing two men who were in debt to the company. He was going to send them to Cape Coast Castle "to be confined in order to bring the rest to reason," but the two men were immediately rescued by their fellow citizens. Astonished by this "insolence," Cruischank punished the rescuers by destroying their houses and exiling them from the town, actions which certainly exceeded his authority. In addition, the "general insolent behaviour of the inhabitants" led the irate Englishman to expend forty pounds of gunpowder in firing at them.[45]

Such displays of arrogance in big things and in small bred a great deal of African resentment against the English. African traders frequently alleged that they were treated unfairly and discourteously by the whites. In 1726 some Liverpool merchants charged that "the inclination of the natives was always more to trade with ships at sea, than with the land factorys, pretty much occasioned by the abuses they receive from those settled amongst them."[46] Despite the merchants' complacency, it would appear that the company and the private traders bore equal responsibility for mistreating their hosts. It is hardly surprising, then, that some Africans retaliated with violent measures. To be sure, not all of the violence directed against the

English could be considered a response to white mistreatment of the African; a good deal of it must have been inspired by the desire for plunder and gain. Englishmen, imbued with a commanding sense of racial superiority, usually denounced all acts of African resistance as mere "insolence."

Kidnapping white traders, sometimes to obtain a ransom, was one way by which the Africans harassed the white men. On occasion, the kidnapped victim would be released after he had been humiliated in some fashion. In 1704 three Royal African Company agents were stripped naked and held prisoner for three days somewhere on the Senegambian coast. Their experience, however mortifying, was better than that of the private trader who was abducted from Anomabo the preceding year. He was kept a prisoner for eighteen days, during which he feared for the loss of his head. The trader bought his release with "good words and a great deal of money." Another trader had a similar experience at the Bight of Benin in 1717. He was imprisoned for three days and was set free only after two chests of arms had been given as a ransom. Captain David Francis's experiences, therefore, were not unique; he reported from James Island fort in 1717 that "my boats and people are seized at almost every port I send them."[47]

Not even the factories and forts were immune from the assaults of disgruntled Africans. In 1701, for example, the factory at Joal in the Gambia was seized by the king, who removed 700 or 800 iron bars (£140 or £160) because a private trader had taken a slave for whom he had not paid. The slave was eventually returned, but the king kept the bars. Two years later black assailants captured the Royal African Company's fort at Sekondi and beheaded the chief merchant. The strongly fortified Cape Coast Castle was attacked by the Asante in 1727, and the battle raged for two days. In 1729 the king of Dahomey assaulted William's Fort in Whydah with a force estimated at 2,000 men.[48]

Though seldom successful, these assaults sometimes did considerable damage to equipment and buildings. Such was the case in September, 1701, when the blacks at Anomabo broke open the outer spur gate at the fort and burnt the outer walls and corn room. The attackers then opened fire on the fort but were driven off after the whites responded with their great guns. Later that night the whites retaliated by setting fire to the "major part of the town." Hostilities continued for twenty-two days, after which the blacks requested a truce, which was mediated by the king of Asebu. The terms of the settlement are not known, but the English reported that the blacks "objected against nothing we proposed them." As evidence of good faith, the blacks "took fetishes [oaths] according to the customs of the country." In addition, they gave their sons as surety to the company "for their better performance of this agreement for payment of the damage done to your Honours' fort." The truce settled nothing, for within a short time the English complained that the blacks had started to "play the old game again, not regarding any agreement that . . . was ever made with them."[49]

Some Englishmen advocated a strong military establishment as one means of providing security. Forts that were adequately weaponed and garrisoned would presumably discourage hostile Africans. James Phipps, an agent at Accra, was convinced that the company "might have a good number of soldiers and slaves to keep the natives in order." The always aggressive Sir Dalby Thomas was one of many agents who yearned to make military conquests in Africa. Thomas believed that Africans could be "kept in awe only by power." He boasted in 1706 that if he had 150 soldiers at Cape Coast, he would destroy the kingdom of Fetu and "foarse" an inland trade. He noted in 1708 that Anomabo "is a nest of villains which ought to be destroyed." His recommendation was the same for the "troublesome" Kabestera. In the next year Thomas growled, "A thousand men fitt for arms, well armed and trained up to it, of Gambia and Whydah slaves, is wanted to subject all these neighbouring countries to our wills and pleasures."[50]

The Royal African Company was perhaps a bit horrified by these proposals for massive military expenditures; the company was financially overextended even at the current level of activity. The court of assistants certainly never contemplated conquering West Africa. It was content to preach the virtues of peaceful trade and leave the men on the spot to make what they could of the situation.

Whether the British trader was primarily interested in selling slaves to his countrymen in the Caribbean or to the Spanish colonists, he faced essentially the same challenges in Africa. There was much ambivalence in the relationship between these white men and their black counterparts. Men of vastly different and to some extent mutually intolerant cultures struggled to cope with each other's manners, idiosyncrasies, and trading practices. Each African group had its own traditions and values, and the English themselves, divided among two chartered companies, Ten Percenters, and miscellaneous interlopers, exhibited much diversity. With European competitors complicating this intricate relationship, the traders lived in an atmosphere of mutual suspicion and doubt. Yet the lure of profit interlocked these aliens, and somehow they learned enough of each other's peculiar ways to work out a basis for successful business enterprise.

NOTES

1. Winthrop Jordan, *White over Black: American Attitudes toward the Negro, 1550–1812* (Baltimore: Penguin Books, 1969), pp. 3–43.

2. PRO, T70/175, pp. 202–10.

3. PRO, T70/170, no folio.

4. PRO, T70/175, pp. 26–27.

5. PRO, T70/175, p. 213.

6. James Houstoun, *Some New and Accurate Observations, Geographical, Natural and Historical . . . of the Situation, Product and Natural History of the Coast of Guinea* (London, 1725), p. 34.

7. PRO, T70/175, pp. 202–10.

8. See, for example, BM, 18272, pp. 27–36.

9. PRO, T70/51, pp. 136–39; T70/52, pp. 170–73, 63–67; T70/68.

10. The European traders had to obtain permission from the local kings to establish a fort or factory. Local rulers also invited the white traders to settle among them. In 1702, for example, the king of Banda sent his nephew to London to invite the Royal African Company to settle in his state, and in 1709 the head caboceers at Ankobra asked the English to build a fort or factory in their territory. See PRO, T70/51, pp. 149–50; T70/5, pp. 7, 61, 64, 67. See also Phyllis M. Martin, *The External Trade of the Loango Coast 1576–1870* (London: Oxford University Press, 1972), p. 75.

11. The best description of the European forts on the West African coast is in A. W. Lawrence, *Trade Castles and Forts of West Africa* (London: Jonathan Cape, 1963).

12. The Royal African Company did not establish a fort on the Loango Coast until 1723, but it was soon destroyed by the Portuguese. See Martin, *External Trade of the Loango Coast*, pp. 81–83. In 1710 the company had five factories on the Gold Coast at Anashan, Shido, Alampo, Tantamkweri, and Egya. The factories on the Gambia were situated at several places, including Barokunda, Bintan, Tankula, Joar, Furbroh, Gereeja, Brefet, Jufureh, Cumbo, and Saalum, See PRO, T70/175, pp. 162–67.

13. Suzanne Miers and Igor Kopytoff, eds., *Slavery in Africa: Historical and Anthropological Perspectives* (Madison: University of Wisconsin Press, 1977), Introduction, pp. 18–26. See also Joseph C. Miller, "The Slave Trade in Congo and Angola," in Martin L. Kilson and Robert I. Rotberg, eds., *The African Diaspora: Interpretive Essays* (Cambridge, Mass.: Harvard University Press, 1976), pp. 76–79.

14. Miers and Kopytoff, *Slavery in Africa*, pp. 12–14, 76–78; Francis Moore, *Travels into the Inland Parts of Africa . . . with a Particular Account of Job Ben Solomon* (London, 1739), in Elizabeth Donnan, ed., *Documents Illustrative of the Slave Trade to America*, 4 vols. (Washington, D.C.: Carnegie Institution, 1930–35), II, 396; BM, 18272, pp. 27–36.

15. William Bosman, *A New and Accurate Description of the Coast of Guinea* (1705; reprinted, New York: Barnes & Noble, 1967), p. 364. The hinterland of Angola may have been an exception to this observation. In his unpublished paper "The Slave Trade and the Jaga of Kasanje," Joseph C. Miller has suggested that a high proportion of the slaves who originated in this area were victims of judicial punishment or of a variety of political decisions. Also see Philip D. Curtin, *Economic Change in Precolonial Africa: Senegambia in the Era of the Slave Trade* (Madison: University of Wisconsin Press, 1975), pp. 153–54.

16. See, for example, J. K. Fynn, *Asante and Its Neighbors, 1700–1807* (Evanston, Ill.: Northwestern University Press, 1971); I. A. Akinjogbin, *Dahomey and Its Neighbours, 1708–1818* (London: Cambridge University Press, 1967). K. Y. Daaku has noted, "It is not without significance that the beginning of the era of the intensive slave trade coincided with the growth of sizeable political entities in the forest regions of the Gold Coast"; see *Trade and Politics on the Gold Coast, 1600–1720* (London: Oxford University Press, 1970), pp. 28–29.

17. PRO, T70/1464, p. 21.

18. PRO, T70/5, p. 74. Walter Rodney has concluded that in the Upper Guinea "localized wars" were fought to obtain slaves for the export market; see *A History of the Upper Guinea Coast, 1545–1800* (London: Oxford University Press, 1970), pp. 102–3.

19. PRO, T70/5, pp. 18, 86.

20. It must be said, however, that the Portuguese who resided at Angola traded regularly for slaves in the interior regions. Herbert S. Klein notes that these traders "established from the beginning thriving urban settlements to control the movement of slaves to the coast and even tried to dominate the interior sources for slaves"; see *The Middle Passage: Comparative Studies in the Atlantic Slave Trade* (Princeton, N.J.: Princeton University Press, 1978), p. 37.

21. William Snelgrave, *A New Account of Some Parts of Guinea and the Slave Trade* (London, 1734), no pagination. Captain William Read reported to the Royal African Company that at Calabar in 1702 Captain Crow, a private trader, had "carried away four negro men after a very unjust sort of manner." A few years later John Crabb, an agent at Komenda, complained that "some of the natives to Windward have been lately carried off by private trading ships." On Nov. 13, 1714, Captain Thirticle of the *Abigail* sailed from Cape Mesurado with eight blacks who had come aboard to trade. According to a Royal African Company agent, Thirticle acted "under pretense of great injuries done him, by having some few goods taken from him when a shore." The captain kidnapped eight more on

Nov. 24 at the River Jong near the cape. One of these men managed to escape by jumping overboard about three leagues from land at about nine o'clock that night and "was in all probability drown'd." See PRO, T70/175, p. 37; T70/5, p. 68; T70/1184, p. 82; T70/6, p. 59.

22. Bosman, *A New and Accurate Description*, p. 475.

23. In 1716, for example, the emperor of Fooni received a boat and five men from the Royal African Company's chief agent at the Gambia in order to "take a place up the river named Geogray [Gereeja?] and to panyar the people and make them slaves." Two years later one Bennett, a factor at Komenda, was accused of encouraging his gunner, presumably an African, to seize black girls and boys "in the bush" for the purpose of selling them clandestinely to interlopers. See PRO, T70/51, p. 104; T70/19, p. 81.

24. PRO, T70/175, pp. 33, 41. In 1703 Captain Meale, a private trader, abducted at Cape Coast Castle an African whom the caboceers had sent aboard his ship to collect customs duties. In retaliation, the Africans seized the ship's surgeon and some of the crew who were on shore. Sir Dalby Thomas mediated the dispute, after which Meale apologized, paid the customs, and released the man; the Africans then freed the whites. The residents at Cape Coast Castle reacted angrily in Oct. 1713, when Captain Hayward, a private trader, abducted eight of the inhabitants. The friends of the kidnapped persons threatened to seize the possessions of the Royal African Company; unfortunately, we do not know the outcome of this incident. See PRO, T70/175, p. 37; T70/5, p. 93.

25. PRO, T70/175, pp. 202–10.

26. Bosman, *A New and Accurate Description*, p. 364; CO, vol. 388, no. 25, 295–96. Curtin cites the case of Waalo, Kajor, and Bawol in the Senegambia, where the ceddo slave-soldiers "were allowed to plunder the peasantry any time the ruler felt the need for foreign exchange to buy European goods, or whenever the ceddo themselves became greedy for booty"; see *Economic Change in Precolonial Africa*, p. 185. For similar practices on the Upper Guinea Coast, see Rodney, *History of the Upper Guinea Coast*, pp. 116–17.

27. Moore, *Travels into Africa*, quoted in Douglas Grant, *The Fortunate Slave* (London: Oxford University Press, 1968), p. 49.

28. Snelgrave, *A New Account*, p. 159; Bosman, *A New and Accurate Description*, p. 364; see also Daaku, *Trade and Politics on the Gold Coast*, p. 29.

29. Moore, *Travels into Africa*, in Donnan, *Documents*, II, 396. For the perversion of the legal process on the Upper Guinea Coast, see Rodney, *History of the Upper Guinea Coast*, pp. 106–8.

30. One recent study of British slave-trading activities on the Gold and Slave coasts during the eighteenth century identifies only nine slaves who were sold for their criminal activities. See S. Tenkorang, "British Slave Trading Activities on the Gold and Slave Coasts in the Eighteenth Century" (M.A. thesis, University of London, 1964).

31. Curtin has shown, for example, that there was no predictable correlation between rising prices and the supply of slaves in the Senegambia during the eighteenth century; see *Economic Change in Precolonial Africa*, p. 168. For a somewhat theoretical discussion of the economic motivations of the slave trade, see Henry A. Gemery and Jan S. Hogendorn, "The Atlantic Slave Trade: A Tentative Economic Model," *Journal of African History* 15, no. 2 (1974), 223–46.

32. Curtin, *Economic Change in Precolonial Africa*, pp. 170, 176. The opposition of some states to the export of slaves from their own nations was a factor that undoubtedly had an impact on supply. In the Senegambia such states included Fuuta Tooro, Gajaaga, and Bundu. See ibid., p. 183.

33. For a discussion of these regions, see Curtin, *Atlantic Slave Trade*, pp. 127–30.

34. These figures were tabulated from the company's record of ships hired. It cannot be stated categorically that all of them were dispatched or that they went to the regions intended. There is no discernible pattern in the destination of the ships prior to 1729. After that year the majority were sent to Angola. This may have been due to a preference for Africans from that region by the residents of Buenos Aires and adjacent areas who received those slaves. On the other hand, it may be explained by favorable supply conditions in Angola in the 1730s. In any event, most of the slave ships that went to Buenos Aires between 1715 and 1738 brought their slaves from Angola.

35. See Davies, *Royal African Company*, pp. 165–79; Rodney, *History of the Upper Guinea Coast*, p. 173.

36. PRO, T70/16, p. 23.

37. For a good discussion of trading practices and the currencies on the African coast, see Marion Johnson, "The Ounce in Eighteenth Century West African Trade," *Journal of African History* 7, no. 2 (1966), 197–214, and her "The Cowrie Currencies of West Africa," *Journal of African History* 11, no. 1 (1970), 17–49; no. 3 (1970), 331–53; see also Curtin, *Economic Change in Precolonial Africa*, pp. 233–57; Daaku, *Trade and Politics on the Gold Coast*, pp. 35–37; Martin, *External Trade of the Loango Coast*, pp. 105–10.

38. Commodities sent from England normally carried a markup of 100 percent in Africa. Thus, if the company anticipated paying an average of £20 per slave in Africa, it would set a ratio of one slave to every £10 of the prime cost of the cargo that was shipped.

39. Snelgrave, *A New Account*, pp. 71, 88.

40. Curtin, *Economic Change in Precolonial Africa*, p. 303.

41. PRO, T70/175, pp. 202–10; T70/23, p. 5. See also Daaku, *Trade and Politics on the Gold Coast*, pp. 18–20; Martin, *External Trade of the Loango Coast*, p. 79. That the English expected kinder treatment from the Africans after presents were distributed is illustrated in the case of the king of Whydah, who received a beaver hat in 1698. The court of assistants optimistically informed the

agents that "this is a fine beaver hat trimm'd with right gold lace and neatly equip't, suppose it will please very well, and that we may reap a considerable benefit by his allegiance." The beaver hat was apparently well received, for five years later, when the Dutch sought permission to build a fort at Whydah, the king refused to grant it unless the resident English agent, Peter Duffield, approved. Duffield hastily reported this triumph over the Dutch and recommended that a present to the king "is in order, a crown may be very proper." See PRO, T70/15, p. 17; T70/13, p. 54.

42. PRO, T70/26, p. 17.

43. The company at one time or another was the ally of the Twifo, Akwamu, Asebu, Dahomey, Fetu, and others. For a discussion of African-European relationships, see Daaku, *Trade and Politics on the Gold Coast*, pp. 48–72; Curtin, *Economic Change in Precolonial Africa*, pp. 121–27.

44. PRO, T70/102, pp. 47–50; T70/1463, p. 12; Daaku, *Trade and Politics on the Gold Coast*, pp. 73–95, 144–81; Akinjogbin, *Dahomey and Its Neighbours*, pp. 39–67.

45. PRO, T70/5, p. 58; T70/7, pp. 104–5.

46. PRO, T70/172, p. 31.

47. PRO, T70/14, p. 70; T70/13, p. 20; T70/19, pp. 70, 86. In 1727 it was reported from Whydah that the blacks "plunder and murder the whitemen at the sand." Also in that year some residents of Cape Mesurado captured a group of traders along with their boat and some goods. The men were released without their boat after paying a suitable ransom. When Whydah was destroyed by the Fon in 1727, all the whites who supported the losing side were captured and taken to Ardra. In 1732 a private trader was killed at Xaaso in the Gambia. This incident was allegedly in retaliation for the ill treatment the Africans had received at the hands of such traders. See PRO, T70/175, p. 36; T70/5, pp. 93, 98; Moore, *Travels into Africa*, in Donnan, *Documents*, II, 409–10.

48. PRO, T70/175, pp. 36, 202–10; T70/5, pp. 70, 93, 98; T70/7, p. 80; T70/172, p. 86.

49. PRO, T70/175, p. 40. The Anomabo were never forced into complete subordination to the whites. For other examples of their resistance throughout the period, see T70/5, p. 42; T70/26, p. 44; T70/6, p. 34; T70/19, p. 78.

50. PRO, T70/5, pp. 40, 43, 47–48; T70/175, pp. 202–10.

3 From Africa to Spanish America

The Atlantic passage seems to have become for later generations the most vivid of all the atrocities of the slave trade. Eyewitness descriptions of slavers' voyages graphically document the suffering of the captives. Yet the individual's ordeal began from the moment he was consigned to slavery on the African continent. The records of the Royal African Company and the South Sea Company provide much information on the slave's odyssey from his African homeland to Spanish America.

Death was present in every stage of the journey. The captives fell victim not only to their indigenous diseases but to the new ones brought by the Europeans. "The natives are incident to our diseases," wrote Sir Dalby Thomas in 1704, noting that they had "the common sort of clapt or poxt [gonorrhea?]," as well as sores and yaws.[1] The proportion of slaves who died between the time of their capture and their delivery to the coast cannot be determined. It is known, however, that of every group of captives several succumbed before being sold, some from disease and others from wounds received at the time of capture. Dead bodies marked the routes to the coast, a prey for scavengers. The Royal African Company's factors frequently reported that some of their slaves had been "buried on the road," an indication that they had died en route to the coast. Of three groups of slaves purchased by the agent at Whydah between 1705 and 1706, the first lost nine on the road, the second eight, and the third nine.[2]

Many slaves who reached the coast died before setting foot on a ship. It was customary to house them in an underground dungeon, variously called a "trunck" or a "hole," in order to reduce the possibility of escape. As an additional precaution, the slaves were put in irons, which were attached to the feet or the neck. In 1708 Sir Dalby Thomas was moved to observe that "the double irons are too painful for the slaves."[3]

The "trunck" in which the slaves were confined, particularly the one at Cape Coast Castle, was exceedingly damp. The captives died in such numbers as to arouse the concern, even the ire, of the Royal African Company. The officials in London, convinced that their employees on the coast were careless, blamed them for the high mortality rates. In 1718 the surgeon at Cape Coast Castle suggested some ways to reduce the deaths among the slaves. His proposals provide a glimpse, albeit indirectly, of the ghastly conditions in the Royal African Company's most important "trunck." He proposed to build special quarters for sick slaves, a sound suggestion in view of the recurring smallpox epidemics. He also recommended constructing a platform eighteen inches high "in the present trunk or dungeon for the slaves to lay on in the night." The bottom and sides of the "trunck" should be lined with boards, half an inch thick, to protect the slaves from the damp walls. The surgeon thought the dungeon should be "smoaked" once a week, especially in the "sickly seasons," to "refresh and sweeten it." The quarters should be cleaned every morning with lime or lemon juice and "strewed with green herbs." Presumably he thought that citrus juice might reduce the stench in those cramped quarters.

The surgeon recommended that tubs be placed in the dungeon "for the slaves to ease themselves at night." Apparently no containers had been provided hitherto, and, since they were chained, the slaves would have been forced to stand or sit in their own excrement. Concern for sanitation also led the surgeon to suggest that clean troughs or bowls be provided for the slaves' food. It is not clear whether he wanted them to eat from communal troughs or individual bowls.

Another of the surgeon's suggestions was unusual, considering the time and place: the attendants who looked after the slaves should "wash and rub" them daily and "shave and oil them once a week"; he also thought their diet should be similar to what they had been accustomed to. Finally, perhaps to improve morale, the surgeon believed it would be desirable to have "castle slaves" on hand, since they would know and understand the customs and habits of the new arrivals.[4]

The company could see the merit in such suggestions, but for whatever reasons—negligence, indifference, or overwork—the factors never significantly improved the care of the slaves, despite repeated prodding from London. In January, 1721, for example, the court of assistants pointedly reminded the factors at Cape Coast Castle about "the great detriment the slaves' hole is to their healths for want of its being lined and a platform raised . . . so notwithstanding all our care to accept of none but choice slaves from any of your factories, yet we have lately had a great mortality, besides a number of them very much reduced and in a bad state of health." A year later it warned James Phipp, captain general at Cape Coast Castle: "We think ourselves obliged to observe to you, that provided the lodgments are kept sweet and clean and the negroes well looked after, and that due care be taken of them, we might expect the danger of mortality is not like to be so great."[5]

In December, 1722, the company explored a grandiose plan for holding the slaves at Cape Coast Castle above ground, hoping thereby to reduce the death rate. A building for the purpose was to be erected on the castle grounds or, as the letter said, "without the castle." The structure was to be about 100 feet square, enclosed by a wall some fourteen or fifteen feet high. Within the enclosure would be accommodations for the slaves, an area for cooking their food, and lodgings for the African attendants who cared for the slaves. The company hoped that these new quarters would allow "the vaults in which they have been kept hitherto [to be] converted to the keeping [of] liquors and other goods which may properly be kept underground." The agents apparently did nothing; there is no evidence that such a building was ever erected. Not until August, 1729, was the company gratified by the steps being taken at Cape Coast Castle to reduce mortality among the slaves, which the company felt had been "occasioned by the dampness of the trunk in which they were kept." Unfortunately, we do not know what corrective measures were finally adopted.[6]

The problem of proper care for the slaves occurred in every company settlement. The court of assistants was preoccupied with Cape Coast Castle because most of the slave shipments were handled there, but it grumbled about other places as well. In 1728 it blamed the high mortality rate of the slaves at the Gambia on "the want of due care in lodging and dyeting them." To the authorities in London it was a matter of angry incredulity that at times the death rate of the slaves on the coast approximated the mortality during the passage to the Americas. As the court of assistants tartly noted, "We cannot but observe, that if slaves can be preserved in their voyage on shipboard, where their best accommodations are but bad and incommodious, their health may certainly be better preserved on shore where clean lodging, fresh air and good dyet will be of more service to them than physick, and therefore we do recommend it to you, as we have often done before that due care be taken of their lodging and dyet, and we doubt not but there will be less occasion for a doctor."[7]

As a means of minimizing losses and speeding the departure of ships, the Royal African Company encouraged its factors to have slaves on hand ready for shipment. This was a dangerous practice, however, for life in the truncks was as hazardous as the Atlantic passage. Sir Dalby Thomas, for one, doubted the wisdom of such a policy; as he expressed it in 1705, "The prime cause of slaves' mortality is buying them before ships arrive." The agents knew they would be blamed whether they had slaves dying at the settlements or if they acquired them as needed and delayed the ships. This dilemma was never resolved; each trader seems to have followed his own intuition, regardless of the wishes of his superiors in England.[8]

The African weather, depending on the time of year, could upset any trader's plans. The annual rainy season, falling roughly between June and August, brought death to whites and blacks alike, and it was unwise to have slaves on hand during that period. Many slaves developed "fevers" from which they would later die during the voyage. Ships that arrived during that season, either by chance or design, ran grievous risks of suffering appreciable losses. The unhappy case of the *George*, which arrived in Buenos Aires in 1717 having lost all but 98 of its cargo of 594 slaves, was not unique. The South Sea Company blamed the disaster on "the length of the voyage and the badness of the weather," adding that "this is not the single instance of that kind." But the rainy season was not always easy to avoid, occurring as it did at different times in different places. After the *Asiento* had endured a particularly disastrous voyage in 1725, the South Sea Company conceded that since the rainy season varied so much, "it can't be expected it can always be avoided."[9]

Sick slaves received medical care, such as it was, from a company doctor—if there was one. From time to time the Royal African Company tried to learn what treatment the Africans themselves used for illnesses. As early as 1699 the factors at the River Sherbro were told to "keep friendship with some natives that understand the best remedies for their distempers."[10] Africans had many kinds of traditional remedies for disease. At the turn of the eighteenth century William Bosman reported from the Gold Coast that lime juice, malagueta pepper, cardamon (an East Indian spice), several varieties of herbs, and the roots, branches, and gums of trees were "the chief medicaments." He found the local remedies "very successful" in their results and was amazed at the "strange efficacy" of the herbs with which "the negroes cure such great and dangerous wounds."

Bosman deplored the fact that European physicians had not bothered to study African herb lore in order to understand "their Nature and Virtue." He felt sure that those herbs "would prove more successful in the Practice of Physic than the European Preparations." [11]

The English were evidently less enthusiastic about the efficacy of African traditional medicine. As might be expected, Sir Dalby Thomas sneered that he had issued "directions to all the factories to enquire after drugs . . . but the blacks, even those that are Trafficquers are so stupid and so ignorant, know nothing thereof . . . all their cures are by Fettish men." [12] These observations notwithstanding, apparently some English physicians utilized African herbs in treating certain diseases. Dr. Houstoun reported:

> What Dispensary Herbs came under my Cognizance in this Place, are Calamus Aromaticus, Serpentana, but much inferior to the Virginian; the Roots of which Herbs I infus'd in Brandy, of which I took a Drachm now and then . . . and gave it as a Cordial to the Sick . . . a pleasant Bitter and good Stomatick, but restricting the relaxed Fibres of the Stomach. I likewise found some Herbs of the Emollient kind resembling Mallows [okra?] and Marsh-Mallows, and the flower of an Herb much resembling our Canomil, which I made use of for emollient Fomentations and Cataplasms. There is a leaf of a Dwarf Tree or Shrub much resembling our Bay Leaf, made use of by the Natives and our White People in the hot Bath with wonderful good Success. [13]

Losses on the African continent represented only the first installment of death: many more persons would die during the Atlantic passage. The kind of voyage that a cargo of slaves endured depended partly upon the care they received from the captain and crew. The typical crew of a British slaver comprised an amorphous group of men. The unemployed and the unemployable who drifted to the seaports might sign on simply to survive. Love of adventure may have attracted others. There were even some men from well-to-do families who became sailors expecting to advance to the higher ranks in the ship's hierarchy or to become traders. Some Bristol merchants pointed out in 1726 that "a great number of the present traders are sons of gentlemen of the best estate and fortunes who have survived their apprenticeship to Masters." [14]

Crew members ranged in age from fourteen to fifty, although there was an occasional older man. Most were young, however, in their late teens or early twenties. The captains and mates, usually older men, had spent more years at sea and presumably had gained experience in the specialized business of trading for and handling slaves. Sir Dalby Thomas, experienced in the business, advised the Royal African Company in 1706 not to hire fastidious officers. "Your Captains and Mates should be such as will do the meanness [*sic*] office, must neither have dainty fingers nor dainty noses, few men are fit for those voyages but them that are bred up to it. It's a filthy voyage as well as a labourious." [15]

The captains faced enormous disciplinary problems with their often unruly crews. Sometimes a ship would be detained in port when part of its crew suddenly decided not to report for duty. In 1716 many of the forty men who had signed on the *Thomas and Deborah*, a South Sea Company vessel, jumped ship. Two years later Captain Foot of the *Asiento* and Captain Spelt of the *Wright* (both South Sea Company ships) reported similar problems. [16] Sailors were also liable to desert once the ship reached Africa. The often long wait on the coast for cargo, the reduction in their numbers caused by deaths, and the contemplation of the awful passage to the Americas must have contributed to the incidence of desertion.

The first task assigned the crew on the coast was to see that the slaves were securely chained in the hold. The males—generally more to be feared than the females—were chained in pairs, the right ankle of one connected to the left ankle of the other; sometimes additional fetters would be fastened to their wrists. Women were treated similarly, although if only a few were aboard, they might be left unfettered. It is unlikely that pregnant women were fettered, but one cannot be sure. Many consignments of slaves included pregnant women and a number gave birth during the Atlantic passage; others delivered their babies after reaching the Americas. Between 1714 and 1718, for example, twenty-five babies were born of slave women within a few days of their arrival at Cartagena. Quite a few infants or "suckling" children were shipped along with their mothers. They were most likely two years old or under and, according to African custom, were still breast-fed. Apparently it was customary not to chain young boys and girls (probably under age ten), since they were no threat to security. [17]

In theory, a ship's tonnage determined the number of slaves it could carry; in practice, a ship sailed with as many as the captain or the owner dictated. Not until 1788 did the British government set a requirement of .6 of a ton per slave for vessels of 160 tons or less built for the slave trade, and .66 of a ton for larger ships. For ordinary ships used in the trade, the ratio was fixed at one slave per ton. [18] The Royal African and South Sea companies seem to have allocated .62 of a ton per slave on their ships; at least this was the average on thirty ships dispatched by these companies between 1713 and 1725. These ships, with a combined weight of 7,837 tons, were registered for 12,590 slaves.

The ratio of .62 of a ton per slave, however, obscures a great deal; some vessels did not take on all the slaves for which they were registered, and others were overloaded. The *Martha*, of 250 tons' burden, went to the Gambia for 400 slaves but sailed with only 200. Similarly, the *Chandos*, of 240 tons' burden, expected to collect 500 slaves in Jakin in 1721 but left with only 417.[19] On the other hand, the 120-ton *Margaret* went to Africa in 1721 for 200 slaves and departed with 265, thus dropping the ratio from .6 to a low .45 of a ton per slave. The case of the *Helden*, a frigate of 202 tons' burden, was even worse: it sailed for Cabinda in 1723, registered for 400 slaves, but actually took on 457. By the time the *Helden* reached Jamaica after a slow passage lasting over three months, 101 slaves had died. Its ratio of .5 of a ton per slave would have been bad enough, but the actual ratio of .44 may have added to the high mortality rate.[20]

There was never any doubt among contemporaries that overcrowding caused deaths. In 1704 agent Thomas Weaver at James Island complained to the Royal African Company that the space allotted per slave on the *Postillion* was too small. "The slaves are so large, [and] it being the general opinion that the slaves could not be healthy in the space of three foot, they broke up one of the platforms which was the reason she couldn't carry more than 100 slaves." Sir Dalby Thomas opposed overcrowding as bad for business, pointing out in 1704 that the practice "will occasion a great mortality." And again, in 1706, he cautioned the company not to "fill your ships too full of slaves."[21]

From time to time the company warned its West Indian agents not to send for more slaves than their ships could accommodate adequately. In June, 1708, the company rebuked its Antigua agent for dispatching a sloop for more slaves than it could carry well: "We take notice you are fitting out the sloope Flying Flame for the coast for 140 negroes, Sir Dalby affirmes you are very much in the wrong to crowd your sloopes so very full of negroes—this very sloope you designed last time should take in 150, Sir Dalby put aboard but 120 which was as many as she was fit to take in and she lost but six." The letter also recalled Thomas's complaint that the *Mary*, which the agent had sent to carry 200 slaves, "is not so big as our ship the Dorothy which was at the same time on the coast and the captain would not take in more than 140 slaves."[22]

Clearly, agents in the West Indies, who were paid on a commission basis, habitually registered their ships for more slaves than the tonnage warranted, gambling against long odds with the slaves' lives. The court of assistants tried to outmaneuver the incorrigible agents by its instructions to the factors in Africa. In 1712 it advised the factors at Cape Coast Castle to dispatch the ships quickly, "though not with their full complement of negroes if upon a survey you find the ship is appointed to take in more negroes than she can conveniently stow. Pray lade no more than are necessary to prevent mortality which has often happen'd by crowding the ship with too many negroes." [23]

The hold of a slaver was a perfect disease environment. Smallpox, measles, scurvy, a variety of "fevers," the bloody flux" (dysentery), and ophthalmia were the most prevalent afflictions. Many of the slaves carried contagion (especially smallpox) aboard from the truncks in Africa. The *Oxford*, for example, docked in Jamaica on January 24, 1713, after three months and two days at sea, having lost 95 of the 521 slaves put aboard at Whydah. The agent in Jamaica reported that "the great mortality was owing to the small pox which went quite through the ship, not a slave escaping it." The experience of the *Indian Queen* in 1716 was even worse: 140 slaves died during the voyage, and the ship reached Buenos Aires with 45 others in advanced stages of smallpox and another 43 just beginning. [24]

Dysentery was another illness to be reckoned with on almost all slave ships. Of the two varieties of dysentery, bacillary and amoebic, the former was more prevalent in the tropics and more deadly. Contaminated food and water cause dysentery; thus the frequent outbreaks of this disease during the Atlantic passage are a positive indication of the unsanitary conditions aboard slavers. Worse still, dysentery often appeared in conjunction with outbreaks of other diseases. The *Queen Anne* arrived in Jamaica in May, 1708, after losing more than seventy slaves to smallpox and dysentery. The following year the Royal African Company's agents at Barbados lamented that many of the slaves in a recent cargo were dying, "they being far gone in the flux and scurvy." In 1714 the *Woolsey* lost twenty-six slaves to dysentery and other diseases in its passage to Jamaica. [25]

There were reported outbreaks of measles during the passage, and some slaves contracted so-called "ship colds," which were accompanied by a high fever and were sometimes fatal. And of course malaria was always present. In 1715 the *Europe* reached Buenos Aires with twenty slaves ill with malaria, and the *Wiltshire* brought sixteen. Even the slaves who escaped illness during the voyage often landed in a terrible condition. The physical and psychological traumas of the Atlantic passage are apparent in agent John Huffam's description of a cargo of slaves delivered to Nevis in

1714: "[They] were very feeble and weak at their landing and many having such a contraction of nerves by their being on board and confined in irons that [they] were hardly capable to walk. . . ."[26]

Both the Royal African and South Sea companies paid close attention to the feeding of their slaves during the passage. Experience had taught the traders that slaves did better when they were fed their customary food, although some English foods were acceptable. In 1705 the Royal African Company's factors at Whydah recommended corn, yams, malagueta pepper, and palm oil as suitable items for the slaves' diet. In addition, they endorsed beans, bread, cheese, beef, and flour brought from England.[27] All the slave ships carried, in varying amounts, some or all of these foods; some also stocked potatoes and rice. To minimize the onset of scurvy, thoughtful captains laid in a good supply of limes and lemons. And if the slaves were lucky, there would be extras or "refreshments" such as plantains, coconuts, malt liquor, rum, and brandy. Sometimes tobacco and pipes were provided. In 1714 the *Norman*, a Royal African Company ship, left London with the following supplies for the 300 slaves it was intended to carry: 150 gallons of malt liquor; 15 bushels of salt; 11½ hogsheads of vinegar; 300 pounds of tobacco; 10 gross of pipes; 4 puncheons of old beef; 3 hundredweight and 10 pounds of flour; 12 hundredweight of biscuits; and 40 quarters of beans.[28]

Each trader calculated the amount of provisions he thought adequate, based on the number of slaves to be carried and the projected duration of the voyage. In 1707 the Royal African Company advised its agents at Cape Coast Castle that for those of its ships that had taken on a supply of beans in England they should add in Africa fifty chests of corn, forty pounds of malagueta pepper, twenty gallons of palm oil, two bushels of salt, and twenty gallons of rum for each hundred slaves. When the South Sea Company contracted with the Royal African Company to "slave" one of its ships in 1723, the contract required that 14 bushels of salt, 280 chests of corn, 170 pounds of malagueta pepper, and 70 gallons of palm oil be put aboard in Africa for the 340 slaves.[29] The guidelines established by the Royal African Company in 1707 were not followed in every detail. When a crucial item such as corn was scarce, the factors had to buy substitutes, and sometimes it was more expedient to provide a cargo of slaves with foods to which they were accustomed. Thus, depending on the ethnic composition of the cargo, yams or rice could replace corn as the staple food.

Although company functionaries in England realized the necessity of providing sufficient food for the slaves, many of their employees in Africa evidently cared very little about the matter. Copious evidence proves that many slaves fared badly in both the quantity and the quality of their food. Shortages regularly occurred aboard the ships. A voyage that lasted more than eight or ten weeks invariably ran short of provisions, leading to rationing and even starvation. The case of the *Dorothy*, which reached Barbados in June, 1709, is typical. That ship brought only 100 slaves after suffering a "great mortality" en route. The company's agent at Barbados attributed the deaths to "povertie for want of provisions, as beefe, oyle, malagetta etc." The *Windsor*'s experience in 1716 was equally tragic: by the time it arrived at Buenos Aires from Angola, there was no food left. The *Windsor* had gone for a cargo of 380 slaves but delivered only 164, and five of these died shortly after their arrival.[30]

Nearly all of the controllable factors governing slave mortality—adequate food, loading only to capacity, exercise, and so on—depended upon the attitude and competence of the captain and his crew. Sir Dalby Thomas was no doubt correct when he said in 1706 that the trader who was familiar with the ways of Africans "shall have his negroes live and do well, when the others that are unacquainted with the method of managing them shall have theirs sickly with great mortality." Sir Dalby also realized that the slaves must be well clothed and fed and kept clean: "Notwithstanding all the care that can be taken both in Europe, Africa and America, if the Captains, mates, surgeons and cooks are not honest, careful and diligent and see that the slaves have always their victuals, well drest, well fed, well washt, cleanly kept and kindly used, the voyage will not be worth a farthing." He ended on a note of hyperbole: "When your ships have great mortality unless occasioned by the smallpox, you may be assured it's through carelessness of your captains, mates, surgeons and cooks usage."[31]

The captain, obviously, bore the primary responsibility for the care of his cargo. He had to acquire the provisions for the slaves and keep his crew from pilfering them. He must make sure that the slaves were fed at the appointed times—generally twice a day—and that the food was well prepared and suited to the slaves' eating habits. It should be mentioned that the female slaves generally assisted in preparing the food on shipboard, perhaps because they knew best the eating habits of their fellows and also because they freed the crew from the chore of cooking.

At least in terms of adequate food, the slaves seem to have fared best on ships that were owned by the captains themselves. Owner-captains had a bigger personal stake in the undertaking, since the more slaves kept alive and in good condition the greater the profit. Of course, the profit motive could work the other way: traders could overcrowd their ships, gambling on a healthy voyage or even assuming that a high mortality would still leave a larger number to sell. It is not very useful to argue whether most traders did or did not practice overcrowding; the evidence for either case simply does not exist, given the absence of the private traders' records.

It is nevertheless true that the slaves brought by private traders often appeared in much better condition than company slaves. Clearly, the captains and crews in the employ of the Royal African Company took indifferent care of their slave cargoes. For example, in February, 1702, the Royal African Company issued a typical complaint to its factors at Barbados: "Our factors at Jamaica complain of a great mortality and meagerness of the negroes by the Sumers Frigat but say they were young and had been lusty and strong when put aboard but charge the whole neglect upon the marriners taking no better care of them."[32]

The survival of some of the shipping records makes it possible to make a rough calculation of the mortality rate aboard the ships for certain periods. The rate varied from ship to ship, of course, depending on such factors as luck, the disease environment from which the slaves came, and the kind of care provided. The death rate was also related to the sailing time to the Americas. Ships that were slaved in East Africa, for example, invariably lost a high proportion of their slaves.[33] Klein's study of the mortality rates of ships carrying slaves to Rio de Janeiro between 1825 and 1830 provides important insights into this phenomenon. He notes that the mortality rates in his sample "seem to be highly correlated with sailing time and port of origin in Africa." The higher mortality rates of slaves from East Africa, according to Klein, "seem consistent with their longer sailing time." Curtin reached a similar conclusion in his analysis of a number of slave voyages to Brazil between 1817 and 1843.[34]

There is a complete set of statistics extant on the number of slaves the Royal African Company carried and the number that died during the years 1680–88. A total of 194 ships left Africa during these nine years, with 60,783 slaves on board. Of this number, 14,388 (23.7 percent) died during the passage, but the decline in mortality over the decade is very noticeable. Table 3 gives a breakdown of these totals.

Between 1700 and 1725 the death rate declined still further to an average of about 13 to 15 percent. The company estimated in 1707 that 15 percent of all its slaves died between the time of purchase and delivery in the New World. In 1713, a particularly good year, of the 2,541 slaves dispatched in nine ships, only 266 (10.5 percent) died.[35] The company's rec-

TABLE 3. Mortality Rate of Slaves Carried in Royal African Company Ships,
1680–88

Year	Number of Ships	Number of Slaves Shipped	Number of Slaves Delivered	Number of Deaths	Percentage of Deaths
1680	17	5,190	3,751	1,439	27.7
1681	18	6,327	4,989	1,338	21.1
1682	21	6,330	4,494	1,836	29.0
1683	28	9,081	6,488	2,593	28.6
1684	17	5,384	3,845	1,539	25.6
1685	29	8,658	6,304	2,354	27.2
1686	28	8,355	6,812	1,543	18.5
1687	18	5,606	4,776	830	14.8
1688	18	5,852	4,936	916	15.6
Total	194	60,783	46,395	14,388	23.7

SOURCE: PRO, T70/175, p. 15.

ords for the years 1720–25 indicate that thirty-three ships sailed for the
West Indies carrying 9,949 slaves. These ships delivered 8,638 of their cargoes alive, losing 1,311 (13.2 percent). Table 4 shows the number dispatched each year and the attendant mortality rates.

It is tempting to speculate on the reasons for the decline in the death
rate for the slave cargoes shipped by the Royal African Company in the
eighteenth century. The slaves most likely received better care, the diet
may have improved, and the ships were possibly being kept in a more sani-
tary condition. In addition, the construction of better and faster ships may
have reduced the sailing time of the voyages.

The data available for other nations provide interesting comparisons
for the British trade. Between 1713 and 1777 the mortality rate on the
ships in the service of the Nantes traders amounted to an average of 12
percent. In the case of the Dutch ships, the death rate between 1680 and
1749 has been calculated at 16.8 percent. There seems to have been a significant decline in mortality in the late eighteenth and the nineteenth centuries. Between 1795 and 1799, for example, an average of 7.7 percent of
the slaves died in the Portuguese trade to Rio de Janeiro, while in the early
years of the nineteenth century the corresponding figure was 9.3 percent.
For British ships that brought slaves to the West Indies between 1791 and
1797, the death rate for the slaves averaged only 5.7 percent.[36]

TABLE 4. Mortality Rate of Slave Cargoes on Royal African Company Ships, 1720–25

Year	Number of Ships	Number of Slaves Shipped	Number of Slaves Delivered	Number of Deaths	Percentage of Deaths
1720	2	579	519	60	10.4
1721	5	1,382	1,187	195	14.1
1722	11	2,948	2,555	393	13.3
1723	11	3,546	2,932	524	15.2
1724	3	1,084	980	104	9.6
1725	1	500	465	35	7.0
Total	33	9,949	8,638	1,311	13.2

SOURCE: PRO, T70/1233, no folio.

Although the majority of persons who died during the Atlantic passage were black, the white crew members also experienced dramatic losses. "It's a melancholy thing," lamented the Royal African Company in 1702, "that the masters of our ships, so many of them dye." No statistics are available on the proportion of the crews that died, but fragmentary evidence suggests that the Atlantic passage was as lethal to crews as to slaves. The Council of Trade and Plantations noted in 1704 that when the slavers arrived in the West Indies "one half of the ship's crew are disabled by sickness." There was hardly a ship that did not lose several crew members. When the *Pindar* arrived in Barbados in May, 1710, the company's agent there indicated that the most noteworthy aspect of the voyage was that "no whiteman died."[37]

The majority of the ships were not so fortunate. The case of the *Royal Africa*, which reached Barbados in February, 1704, after losing nineteen of its crew, was not considered unusual. The following year a ship reached Nevis "with all the whitemen except 9 dead." The *Queen Elizabeth*, which docked at Barbados in 1714, had left Sierra Leone in 1712 and "had been 15 months on her voyage and lost 5 Captains." And during the *Indian Queen*'s journey from Africa to Buenos Aires in 1716, sixteen crew members died.[38] As in the case of the slaves, the death rate among the crew seems to have declined as the eighteenth century wore on. During the 1780s the mortality rate of the crews on 112 vessels in the English slave trade averaged about 22 percent per voyage. For a similar group of men in the Nantes slave trade between 1712 and 1777 the death rate stood at 18.3 percent.[39]

In spite of the fact that the slaves were shackled and often debilitated by disease during the Atlantic passage, there can be no doubt that many of them resorted to violence in their attempts to liberate themselves. Slave trader William Snelgrave recounted several incidents of voyages during which mutinies had occurred, resulting in either the loss of ship and crew or in the death and wounding of many slaves. As ship's surgeon John Atkins wrote: "There has not been wanting examples of rising and killing a ship's company distant from land, tho' not so often as on the coast."[40]

Most rebellions did not result in the total loss of the cargo, but frequently they ended in a serious loss of life among the slaves. A few examples will suffice. In an uprising on the *Tiger*, sailing from the Gambia in 1702, about forty slaves and two crew members were killed. The frigate *Urban* had even greater losses when its slaves mutinied in May, 1703: the crew killed twenty-three men and wounded another twenty men and one boy. A few months later the slaves on the *Martha*, bound from Whydah to Nevis, also rose. According to a report, the sailors "fired on them and killed 2 very lusty men and afterwards they were highly peaceable." The ship had 273 slaves on board at the time. The *Dorothy* also experienced an uprising in its passage from Cape Coast Castle to Barbados the following year. The details are scant, but it is known that several wounded slaves received medical attention in Barbados. And in 1707 three slaves on the *Sherbro*, bound from Sierra Leone to Barbados, were shot during an uprising.[41]

Slaves who could not rebel found other means of resistance. The women, according to Snelgrave, were "the most troublesome to us, on account of the noise and clamour they made." Hunger strikes were sufficiently common that the crews developed standard techniques for compelling slaves to eat. John Atkins recalled that it was customary to "have an overseer with a cat-o-nine tails" to force food on those who baulked. If whipping failed, the slaves could be force-fed with the help of an instrument that held the jaws apart. For more stubborn cases, thumb screws could be applied in order to force compliance.[42]

The mood of deep despair that overwhelmed many of the slaves on board ship led inevitably to the will to death. Traders called this emotional condition a "fixed melancholy," which nothing could dispel. These slaves remained impassive and motionless, refusing all food and drink. Thomas

Butcher, an agent of the South Sea Company at Caracas, reported in 1738 that a number of slaves in a recently arrived cargo were "very lean and thin." When he investigated the reason for their condition, the captain of the ship told him that "there was about 40 of the cargo that were bought out of one ship and put aboard his snow [and] soon after they were put on board the most of them began to fall away and grow thin, notwithstanding the endeavours used to prevent it, and they could never be recovered afterwards." Sixteen of these slaves died shortly after arriving in port.[43] Some of those who manifested this condition had been totally crushed by enslavement; they never regained their mental equilibrium. Then there were others who, having realistically faced their plight and the possibility of worse to come, concluded that death was preferable. In a sense the death wish was one way, however tragic, of regaining control of one's destiny.

The recorded episodes of the Atlantic passage demonstrate how much suffering human beings can endure. At the same time they exemplify the resilience and triumph of the human spirit over adversity. In little ways the African slaves resisted dehumanization and thereby retained a degree of personal dignity under oppression. John Atkins could write that "the women retain a modesty, for tho' stripped of that poor clout which covers their privities they will keep squatted all day long on board to hide them."[44] Many of them, too, in affirmation of their humanity, had fought to liberate themselves. Those who survived had watched their fellow captives die week after week, endured every assault on body and spirit, and yet they had lived to tell their story.

NOTES

1. PRO, T70/28, p. 46.
2. PRO, T70/18, p. 89.
3. PRO, T70/5, p. 49.
4. PRO, T70/1185, no folio.
5. PRO, T70/27, p. 28; T70/53, p. 82.
6. PRO, T70/53, p. 98; T70/54, p. 18.
7. PRO, T70/55, p. 135.
8. PRO, T70/5, p. 8.
9. BM, 25563, pp. 91, 95; 25565, pp. 367, 375.
10. PRO, T70/51, p. 17.
11. Bosman, *A New and Accurate Description*, pp. 224–25.
12. PRO, T70/14, p. 25.

13. Houstoun, *Some New and Accurate Observations*, p. 5.

14. PRO, T70/172, p. 24.

15. PRO, T70/26, no folio.

16. BM, 25498, p. 51; 25555, p. 69.

17. PRO, T70/957, no folio; T70/19, p. 58; Jorge Palacios Preciado, *La trata da negros por Cartagena de Indias, 1650–1750* (Tunja: Universidad Pedagógica y Tecnológica de Colombia, 1973), p. 264.

18. Davies, *Royal African Company*, p. 194. The Portuguese were the first to pass laws governing the ratio of slaves to tonnage. Beginning in 1684, Portuguese laws allowed a ratio of 2.5 to 3.5 slaves per ton, depending on the ship's make. See Klein, *Middle Passage*, pp. 29–30.

19. PRO, T70/1233, no folio.

20. Ibid.

21. PRO, T70/14, p. 66; T70/26, p. 4; T70/5, p. 6.

22. PRO, T70/58, p. 172.

23. PRO, T70/52, p. 139. Modern research has begun to challenge the assertion that overcrowding was the principal cause of the many deaths during the Atlantic passage; see Klein, *Middle Passage*, p. 66; and Herbert S. Klein and Stanley L. Engerman, "Slave Mortality on British Ships, 1791–1797," in Roger Anstey and P. E. H. Hair, eds., *Liverpool, the African Slave Trade and Abolition*, Historic Society of Lancashire and Cheshire, Occasional Series no. 2 (Bristol: Western Printing Services, 1976), p. 118.

24. PRO, T70/13, p. 50; T70/8, pp. 16, 34; Seville, Archivo General de Indias, Indiferente General, vol. 2800 (hereafter cited as AGI, Indiferente). The later records of the colonial officials indicate, however, that when the slaves on the *Indian Queen* were "measured," only 77 appeared to be ill. See AGI, Indiferente, 2809.

25. PRO, T70/8, pp. 33, 55, 85. In its continuing search for the causes of sickness and death aboard the ships, the Royal African Company concluded that changes in diet and water were partly responsible. In 1705 the company told Dalby Thomas that "the Captains and others" had agreed that while the slaves "are at Cape Coast the water they drink is not good and they are kept short of provisions, and upon alteration in both after [they are] put aboard may occasion the heat of the ship to have a greater influence upon them and cast them into their fatall distempers." Contaminated water may have been largely responsible for the gastrointestinal disorders that frequently occurred. By 1706 the company had begun to understand the possible connection between the two. In that year agent Benjamin Bullard at Barbados noted that water stored in rum casks was particularly harmful for drinking. The company passed the information on to Dalby Thomas on the coast: "They find by experience that rum casks are not fit to be filled with water for the negroes to drink, it gives them the gripes, and occations a mortality amongst them, it may do well to boile their food [water?], the fire cor-

rects the ill taste and bad effects of the water." There is no evidence that this advice was followed. See PRO, T70/52, pp. 55, 70.

26. PRO, T70/19, p. 13; T70/18, p. 65; AGI, Contaduría 265, ramos 5, 13; AGI, Indiferente, 2800. It is not clear from the records whether the twenty slaves suffering from malaria on the *Europe* were the only ones who were ill. The slaves on the *Wiltshire* had sores on their bodies as well as malaria.

27. PRO, T70/28, p. 65.

28. Donnan, *Documents*, II, 181.

29. PRO, T70/52, p. 100. A second contract signed later that year required the Royal African Company to supply the 300 slaves aboard the *Francis* with 12 bushels of salt, 240 chests of corn, 50 pounds of malagueta pepper, and 60 gallons of palm oil; see BM, 25567, pp. 5–8.

30. PRO, T70/52, p. 119; T70/8, p. 45; T70/3, p. 59; AGI, Contaduría 268, ramo 1.

31. PRO, T70/26, p. 4.

32. PRO, T70/58, p. 15.

33. The *St. Michael* and the *Sea Horse* lost over 600 of the 1,030 slaves they carried from Madagascar to Buenos Aires in 1727 and 1728 respectively; see BM, 25557, p. 21.

34. Klein, *Middle Passage*, pp. 86–87; Curtin, *Atlantic Slave Trade*, p. 281.

35. PRO, T70/63, no folio.

36. Klein, *Middle Passage*, pp. 161, 64, 83; Klein and Engerman, "Slave Mortality," p. 117.

37. PRO, T70/58, p. 22; CSP, no. 156 (1704–5), p. 64.

38. PRO, T70/1445, p. 11; T70/8, p. 89; AGI, Indiferente, 2800.

39. Curtin, *Atlantic Slave Trade*, p. 284; Klein, *Middle Passage*, p. 194.

40. Snelgrave, *A New Account*, p. 173; John Atkins, *A Voyage to Guinea, Brazil and the West Indies* (London, 1735), p. 175.

41. Donnan, *Documents*, II, 5; PRO, T70/13, pp. 21, 31; T70/890, p. 70; T70/8, p. 30.

42. Snelgrave, *A New Account*, pp. 105–6; Atkins, *Voyage to Guinea*, p. 171.

43. Shelburne MSS, Clements Library, Ann Arbor, Mich., vol. 44, 617–23.

44. Atkins, *Voyage to Guinea*, p. 180.

4 The Structure of the Asiento Trade in the Americas

The arrival of a slave ship in the Americas opened a very different phase of the trading process. For the slaves, memory was the only remaining link with their homeland and their past; the bewildering, unpredictable new life was at hand. Until their sale on the retail market, the captives would be treated as rather valuable commodities whose appearance of health and strength was of prime importance. Of necessity, the chartered companies had to set up organizations in the Americas to manage their business and dispose of their slaves. The Royal African Company had confined its operations to the English islands, but the South Sea Company, in addition to agencies on the islands, possessed factories in the Spanish empire as well.

During the first period of the asiento trade (1714–19) the South Sea Company established agencies in both Barbados and Jamaica. These islands were the greatest receiving points for slavers from Africa. In Barbados and Jamaica the company purchased slaves from private traders and the Royal African Company and received the cargoes from its own ships. To a lesser extent, the company also bought slaves at St. Christopher and from the Dutch at Curaçao and St. Eustatius.

Initially, the South Sea Company regarded Barbados and Jamaica as equally important centers. As the asiento trade became more firmly established, the company realized that Jamaica's volume of business eclipsed that of Barbados. By the time hostilities between England and Spain interrupted trade in 1719, it was evident that the Barbados factory was not necessary and it was quietly abandoned. Although a few ships would be dis-

patched to Spanish America in the company's name from Barbados and St.
Christopher in the 1730s, the agents no longer had permanent residences
on these islands.

To conduct its trade with the Spaniards, the South Sea Company established factories at Cartagena, Buenos Aires, Vera Cruz, Havana, Santiago de Cuba, Porto Bello, and Panama. Porto Bello was not an autono-
mous factory but was under the Panama factory's jurisdiction. The factory
at Santiago de Cuba was small; it had been established to relieve some of
the burden on the Havana factory and to keep closer surveillance on the
contraband trade that flourished all along the Cuban coast. Caracas was
elevated to factory status in 1735 in response to the increased demand for
slaves in Venezuela and adjacent areas.[1]

The staffing of all these factories was not cheap. Agents at Jamaica
and Barbados were paid a commission on the gross sale of slaves in the
two islands, as well as on each slave they shipped to Spain's empire. For
the first ten years of the asiento the other agents at the various factories in
Spanish America received a fixed salary and a subsistence allowance, but
the company eventually decided that its employees needed more incentive.
Accordingly, after 1725 they were paid on commission.[2]

The company also paid stipends to a number of Spanish officials under the terms of the asiento contract. Among these was the president of the
Council of the Indies, the principal administrative agency for the colonies.
He received 2,000 pesos (£450) a year from the company, and his secretary 100. The five members of the Junta de Negros, a council committee
responsible for adjudicating disputes between the company and the Spaniards, each received 600 pesos a year. A few minor functionaries received
yearly stipends ranging between 100 and 300 pesos. The company's own
representative in Madrid received a salary of 2,000 pesos annually.[3]

The Spaniards in the company's service at the various factories were
reasonably well paid. Most expensive were the judges conservators, who
heard and resolved local squabbles between the English and the Spaniards;
their annual salaries ranged from 2,000 to 3,000 pesos, except at Vera
Cruz where the salary was 1,500 and at Santiago de Cuba where it was
800 pesos. Spaniards served as attorneys, marshals, physicians, guards,
stewards, carpenters, supervisors of slaves, and household servants. Their
salaries varied with the factory and the work required. An attorney, for
example, was paid 800 pesos a year at Panama and Porto Bello but only
500 at Havana and 400 at Buenos Aires. In general, most of the other employees received between 100 and 600 pesos annually.[4]

When the asiento trade was resumed in 1722 at the end of the war, the company routed all of its incoming slave ships from Africa directly to Kingston in Jamaica. The only regular exceptions were the two or three ships that went to Buenos Aires annually. To ensure an adequate supply of slaves to Buenos Aires and adjacent areas, such as Chile, the contract stipulated that 1,200 piezas de Indias be landed at Buenos Aires each year. The company decided that the slaves should come directly from Africa on ships hired in England and dispatched from an English port. On the third leg of the voyage the ships could carry to England vast quantities of the hides for which Buenos Aires was justly famous.

The agents in Jamaica (and at Barbados during the time the company was settled there) were responsible for receiving, inspecting, and accommodating the slave cargoes as they arrived from Africa. In the unusual event that the slaves were in good physical condition, they were sent on to Spanish America without delay, either on the original ship or aboard company sloops or packet boats. More commonly, the entire cargo was so debilitated that it had to be landed to recuperate from illness or to be "refreshed" before continuing the journey.

Newly arrived slaves were accommodated in rudely constructed houses and huts within enclosures or "pens" which the company owned or rented. The agents hired local whites and free blacks to care for the slaves, and a physician was on call. To speed their recovery, it was customary to bathe the sick slaves in "sweet herbs," that is, in water in which the leaves of certain plants noted for their therapeutic qualities were either boiled or soaked. Others had their mouths washed out with lime juice, undoubtedly a procedure considered effective in curing scurvy.

The agents made special efforts to feed the slaves well at this time. Twice a day they were fed meals that included beef, rice, flour, yams, biscuits, bread, fish, bananas, and a Barbadian food called canky. There was rum to enliven their spirits, and tobacco and pipes for smoking. The maintenance cost per slave was about 6d. a day, which seems small. Considering that yams and bananas were relatively cheap, that rice and flour sold at 2d. or less per pound, and that fish was less than 3d. per pound, the allowance for food seems to have been adequate.[5]

It is unlikely that the majority of the slaves destined for Spanish America remained in the pens longer than thirty days. There was always the danger of an epidemic, and maintenance costs were not negligible. As soon as the slaves looked salable, the agents shipped them to the factories in Spanish America. Even at the peak of its shipping activities, the South Sea

Company depended on purchases from other traders to get its full quota. For example, of 1,597 slaves that the company shipped from Jamaica between December 5, 1716, and August 3, 1717, the company had to buy 349 (22 percent) to round out the cargoes.[6]

After 1730 the company purchased an even larger proportion of its slaves in Jamaica. In fact, in 1731 the court notified trader Humphrey Morrice that it had resolved "for some time past to depend on the Jamaica market for the provision of all such negroes as their agents shall want for the supply of the Spanish West Indies." In time, the company dominated the market. Agent John Merewether could report in September, 1737, that "the ships from Angola and Calabar bring in three assortments of negroes, the first for the South Sea Company, the second for the planters and the third for the illicit traders." The Gold Coast ships, Merewether added, "import negroes for us and the planters. They are to[o] dear for the traders." But the quality of some of these slaves, the agent complained, was so mediocre that the company purchased only 940 (32 percent) of the 2,907 slaves that had come to the island in the last six months. Even then, said Merewether, "we did not put by one that we thought would please the Spaniards."[7]

The agents were responsible for selling the new slaves who came on the company ships but who were considered unfit for the Spanish market. These "refuse negroes" were purchased by the Jamaican planters for local use or by independent traders who fed them well, nursed them back to health, and then sold them clandestinely to the Spaniards. Between June, 1716, and August, 1718, the agents at Jamaica sold 710 "refuse negroes."[8]

The planters had strong preferences as to the physical appearance of the slaves, particularly the women. Slave owners who demanded sexual favors from the black women purchased the ones they adjudged attractive. The Royal African Company noted in 1704 that the Barbadian masters preferred "young and full breasted" women.[9] The Spaniards seem to have favored slaves who were phenotypically black as opposed to those who were racially mixed. The basis for their preference is not clear; suffice it to say that the South Sea Company cautioned its captains sailing to Madagascar to buy only slaves "of the blackest sort with short curled hair and none of the tawny sort with strait hair." In 1736 agent Merewether wrote from Jamaica that he was selecting only slaves "who are not too much of the yellow cast" for the Cuban market. Thomas Butcher, the agent at Caracas, recommended that slaves sent to that port "be of the finest deep black (Congo and Angola slaves being the best liked here) without cutts in their faces nor filed teeth, the men to be well grown of a middle stature not too tall nor too short . . . the women to be of a good stature, not too short and small without any long breasts hanging down." [10]

Age was also of paramount importance. The preference for slaves in their teens and early twenties was universal, since these were the productive years, in terms of both labor and offspring. As early as 1701 the Royal African Company wrote its agents at Cape Coast: "We are advised from the islands that boys and girls not under twelve years old sell very well. . . . Rather than buy any negroes above the age of 30, supply them with healthy boys and girls." Three years later the company noted that the Barbadians wanted boys of fourteen, fifteen, and sixteen years of age. The court of assistants also scolded its Cape Coast agents about an unsatisfactory cargo of slaves recently arrived in Barbados: the company's employees there complained "of a great many of the men and women that they were old and the women had boarn 3 or 4 children." In 1739 the South Sea Company's agent at Caracas recorded that the male slaves to be sent there were to range in age from "20 to 23 or 24 but none to exceed 25 years of age." The women were to be from "18 to 20 but none to exceed 22 years of age, the boys from 14 to 18 and the girls from 13 to 17 years of age [and there should be] as many men as women, and as many boys as girls, or as near as possible, and all to be well flesh'd and not too thin and lean, for skin and bones only will not sell them." [11]

Under the circumstances the South Sea Company's employees had to be particularly careful in choosing slaves for Spanish America. The Spaniards demanded the best and paid premium prices. According to one observer in 1728, the Spaniards would not buy "sickly and distemper'd negroes," such as those who "want an eye, or toe, a finger, two or three teeth or such whose teeth are filed like a saw." In 1734 the court of directors marveled that "the Spaniards are so nice as to size, colour and want of perfection, that they will reject a negro for want of a tooth, or a nail or for having a yellow cast." Such select slaves were not always easy to obtain. The agents would send the less appealing slaves first, hoping that competition would force the Spaniards to buy them; the choice cargoes arriving later would always sell. When the agents sent two such cargoes to Porto Bello in 1725, the court of directors readily approved "sending the sorts of negroes least coveted first . . . you being certainly right, the greater the demand, the fewer the objections." [12]

The factors at the various Spanish American ports constantly complained about the quality of the slaves. Weary of the subject, the company in 1723 accused the factors at Porto Bello and Buenos Aires of being too discriminating. In particular, the agents at Buenos Aires were informed that if their "extreme nicety were avoided," they would "not doubt of constant supplies and though all of them might not be so very fine as you could wish, yet it would be a means to defeat the private traders of their supplies." The private traders entered into the company's argument in roundabout fashion. The court of directors thought the Jamaica agents rejected too many slaves because of the Spanish American factors' complaints; these "refuse negroes" were bought cheaply by interlopers, fattened up, and sold illicitly to the Spanish. The company hoped to eliminate competition by selling the Spaniards the less desirable slaves, thereby becoming the sole importer of slaves "in deed as well as in name." The company's argument was seriously flawed, since it presupposed that the illicit traders only bought slaves that had been rejected by the company's agents in Jamaica or Barbados. In fact, these traders purchased slaves in all of the islands, and their cargoes were not entirely or even significantly composed of "refuse negroes." [13]

The company's slaves were carried to Spanish America in hired vessels. The owners of ships, sloops, and packet boats were anxious to make these vessels available to the company at a moderate fee. The agents, accordingly, made one of two different types of contracts with the proprietors of these vessels. In the first type the agent hired the vessel for a stated number of months, appointed the captain and crew, and paid the owner a fixed monthly fee. The fee varied with the size of the vessel, the number of slaves it could accommodate, and the amount of Spanish American products (such as cocoa and hides) it could transport to the port of origin. Monthly rental fees ranged between £45 and £200. Thus, in 1735, the sloop *Sea Nymph* was hired to carry 100 slaves from Barbados to Caracas for £45 per month. The larger *Elizabeth*, which transported 200 slaves between the same ports in that year, was chartered at £200 per month. Under this type of contract the company paid the wages of the captain and crew. A captain generally received £10 per month and an ordinary seaman between £3 10s. and £4 10s. monthly. Skilled seamen, such as carpenters and pilots, commanded £6 per month. [14]

The second type of contract appears to have been more commonly used. In this case the company agreed to pay the owner a fixed sum per head for slaves carried to the Spanish empire. To be sure, the freight charges varied depending upon the distance between ports. Slaves were normally transported the short distance from Kingston to Havana at 4 pesos (18s.) or 5 pesos (22s. 6d.) per head; for the longer journey to Cartagena the charge was 5 pesos (22s. 6d.) or 6 pesos (27s.). The company furnished the slaves' food, most often consisting of flour, bread, rice, biscuits, bananas, beans, and salted meat and fish.

Purchasing slaves in the West Indian islands for shipment to Spanish America was not without difficulties. The Jamaicans were never very happy with the South Sea Company's operations. The planters and colonial officials condemned the company's practice of purchasing the choice slaves at high prices. Governor Sir Nicholas Lawes complained in November, 1717, "The Asiento carries all the able, stout and young negroes, or such as they call peic'd India [*sic*] to the Spaniards and sell none to the planters but old, sickly and decrepid, or what are called Refuse, if a choice negro is sold to a planter, he must give as much or more than the Spaniard, and that in ready money." [15] The governor exaggerated, but a year later he was probably right in announcing that the contract "is believed by the people of Jamaica to be . . . injurious to the commerce and prejudicial to the planting interest of the island." The independent traders in Jamaica were also incensed that the company took over their trade with the Spanish Americans under the asiento. [16]

The decline in private trade between the Jamaicans and the Spaniards soon became the subject of spirited pamphleteering. The anonymous author of a 1728 pamphlet, for example, noted that prior to 1713 such traders sold "considerable quantities of British manufactures" to Spain's colonies annually, asserting that a sloop which carried 120 slaves generally brought other merchandise valued at £7,000 or £8,000. The traders had had no difficulty in disposing of their cargoes because "the necessity which the Spaniards were under for negroes before they were so largely supplied by the South Sea Company occasioned the Royal officers to wink at those proceedings." Four years later, in 1732, the Council and Assembly of Jamaica agreed that the asiento had hurt the islanders by stopping "their trade in general to the Spanish settlements." [17]

Not surprisingly, the disgruntled Jamaicans opened a campaign to harass the company and cripple its trade in the island. In 1715 the Assembly began consideration of a motion to impose a duty on all slaves that the company exported to Spanish America. Alarmed, the company sent a strong, although premature, protest to the British government, arguing that such a levy should be annulled, since it would be "burdensome and destructive" to the company's business. [18]

The Assembly formally approved the tax measure in November,

1716. The act levied a duty of £1 on every slave exported from Jamaica, making no distinction between those purchased in the island and those merely transshipped from there. Agents Pratter and Hazelwood wrote the home office that the Assembly thought such exactions were "an easy way of raising money to pay the debts of the country." [19]

As expected, the company again petitioned the crown for repeal of the act. After deliberating, the Council of Trade and Plantations upheld the duty on slaves purchased in the island but ruled against any levy on slaves temporarily landed at Jamaica for "refreshment." "It could not be reasonable that they should lay a tax upon negroes landed there by the South Sea Company for refreshment and much less on such as only put into their harbour for wood and water, because this would be an oppression of the South Sea Company and consequently support Jamaica at the expense of the British trade." [20]

Forced to submit, the Assembly looked around for ways to circumvent the company's obvious advantage at Whitehall. The ingenious Jamaicans soon found a loophole. Their money bills were passed only for one year at a time, so periodically they reimposed the disputed tax and collected the revenue from the company. By the time the crown received a formal petition from the company and nullified the tax, the Assembly could humbly submit that the provision had already expired. By 1724 the South Sea Company was reduced to protesting that it might be "put under the necessity of proceeding with the negroes directly from Africa to the Spanish West Indies without having an opportunity of landing and refreshing them and supplying others in the room of such as may have died in the voyage or contracted sickness which may have rendered them unfit for the Spaniards." Between 1721 and 1725 the agents at Jamaica reported that they had paid £9,086 in export levies and still owed £1,090. [21]

The Jamaicans' campaign was nothing if not inventive. The company drew attention to an ingenious provision of an act that had again placed a duty of £1 per head on all slaves exported from the island. To circumvent the meaning and spirit of the crown's arguments for the earlier nullifications, the new act treated the whole of a ship's cargo as taxable, provided that any part of it was sold locally. The company threw up its hand in horror, and the crown duly annulled the act in 1727. [22]

In 1729 the Assembly levied a duty on slaves, including those "exported [from] though not landed" on Jamaica. This strange measure took in all those slaves who arrived at any harbor en route to Spanish America but who had not disembarked. With a bow toward Whitehall, the Assembly wrote a special exclusion clause: "All negroes or other slaves brought into the island which shall not be sold or disposed of, or the property altered in this island, but shall be exported therefrom, shall be free from all dutys imposed by this act on negro slaves." The key phrase in this masterpiece of misleading legislation was "or the property altered in this island." The company's whole point in landing the slaves for "refreshment" was to "alter" them; hence the exclusion clause neatly left the re-exported slaves subject to the duty. When the crown nullified this act in 1731, the governor of Jamaica was instructed not to assent to any such laws in the future "on pain of His Majesty's highest displeasure and being recalled." Such threats did not deter the Assembly from imposing the prohibited taxes year after year only to have them annulled. In 1734 the Assembly tried out a new justification for the duties; in a petition to the Council of Trade and Plantations, the governor argued that the economic "distress" on the island necessitated the imposition of such taxes.[23]

Although the company was irritated by the exactions of the Assembly, it never seriously considered leaving Jamaica. As early as 1716 the company resolved to stay and fight for its interests while recognizing, as the court of directors put it, "that the people of Jamaica are set against the Company and will do them all the disservice they can and constrain us thereby to seek for other means to supply the Spanish coast with negroes than by way of that island." The court of directors reacted to the Assembly's harassment by launching a propaganda campaign. In 1728 agent James Rigby published a lengthy vindication of the company's conduct of the asiento and listed the advantages to Jamaica of the company's presence there.[24]

The company was convinced that it had enriched the island's economy. In 1732, for example, it insisted that slave merchants were drawn to Jamaica by "an expectation of a double market," that of the planters and that of the company. Such a profusion of traders gave the planters "an opportunity of supplying themselves with negroes on better terms and to sell their produce at a better price." The slave ships spent "great sums" in the island, thereby creating employment. The company rejected the notion that the asiento contract had destroyed the islanders' trade with the Spaniards, since everyone knew that such trade relations were still active. In any event, the court of directors added solicitously, "The trade which the Company is charged with wresting from the island was trade conducted in a clandestine manner at great peril to those who conducted it."[25]

The company's most lengthy self-justification appeared in the memo-

rial presented to the Council of Trade and Plantations in 1734. The council was invited to consider the company "a corporation carrying on a trade
under a national contract . . . for the advantage of Great Britain." As a
national institution it should receive "all possible encouragement," particularly from the ungrateful Jamaicans. There followed an exhaustive discussion of the many benefits conferred upon Jamaica by the company's
presence. It was the usual list, with one or two new twists added. The company denied the charge that its purchase of choice slaves left only the refuse for the Jamaicans. Since the Spaniards were so selective, the leftovers
must still be very desirable. Besides, "the Company refusing such negroes
leaves a greater plenty and at a lower rate for the planters." Why should
the company contribute to the financial support of the island? It owned no
land or plantations there. Nor should the Jamaicans tax the company's
slave purchases; such an exaction was like making "a passenger in an inn
at a thoroughfare town contribute to the parish rates."[26]

The company and the Jamaicans were never able to resolve their differences. The Jamaican traders never forgave the company for depriving
them of some of their illicit trade to the Spanish colonies. The planters
could not ignore the fact that the company not only bought the best slaves
but that its presence tended to inflate prices. The Assembly, reflecting the
resentment of its constituents, erroneously believed the company to be
enormously wealthy and hence able to absorb painlessly the various levies
imposed upon it. On the other hand, the company never made any serious
attempts to ingratiate itself with the Jamaicans or to counteract its image
as the rich, powerful outsider, one that it retained throughout the asiento
period. Its difficulties with the Jamaicans were therefore partially of its
own making.

Despite the problems with the Assembly and the people, the company
was able to carry on its business in Jamaica as effectively as its abilities and
finances permitted. The factors on the island—men like Edward Pratter
and James Rigby—were deeply committed to the company's best interests,
not to mention their own commissions. The company's confidence in these
men led in 1725 to their being put in charge of all the factories in Spanish
America. It became their responsibility to supervise the operation of these
factories, to coordinate and satisfy their needs, and to receive their reports
and financial statements.

As a means of identifying the slaves and reducing the number of illicit
operations, the company required its factors in Spanish America to brand
or, more euphemistically, "mark" the slaves they sold. Unmarked slaves

were assumed to have been brought in illicitly and were subject to confiscation. Each factory had its own brand, usually a replica of its initials. In the early years of the trade a replica of the company's arms was also branded on the slave, but this practice seems to have been used less frequently as the years wore on. The branding iron was made of gold or silver. The traders preferred gold irons because they were said to make a sharper, more distinctive scar.[27]

To prevent theft or duplication, the company recommended keeping each branding iron secured by three locks; only the most important and trustworthy men at the factory were to have access to the keys. When a branding iron was stolen or lost, as sometimes happened, the replacement bore a different design. Thus one factory may have used two or three different brands during the asiento period. The branding operation was simple but painful. In 1725 the court of directors noted that the technique used "is to mark the negroes on the left shoulder, heating the mark red hot, and rubbing the part first with a little palm or other oil, and taking off the mark pretty quick, and rubbing the place again with the oil."[28]

At the factories in Spanish America the slaves were housed in buildings, or "negrorys," rented for that purpose. A serious attempt was generally made to feed them well in order to build up their resistance to disease and to make them more salable. Their diet was similar to that in the islands and on shipboard: beef, fish, rice, bread, flour, and bananas. Some of these items, such as flour and rice, had been brought from the Caribbean in the slave ships.

Most Spanish customers came to the factories to buy slaves, but some, such as those who lived in the interior of large colonies like Mexico, would not normally make the journey to the coast to buy a slave or two. The English factors quickly realized that they could expand their trade if they took their slaves to the remoter areas. This was easier said than done; royal officials looked askance at Englishmen going to the hinterland. They feared that the traders would use the opportunity to engage in contraband trade or spy on the empire. In urging the exclusion of Englishmen from the interior of Mexico and Peru, the archbishop of Mexico in 1725 suggested that "they might be our enemies in the future." Since the asiento contract permitted no more than six English traders to reside at a factory at any one time, it is hard to see their threat to Spanish security. Objections like the archbishop's reflected anti-English prejudice more than a realistic assessment of the pros and cons of allowing a few Englishmen access to the interior.[29]

The controversy over whether the English should be permitted inland raged sharpest at Buenos Aires. Article 9 of the asiento contract stipulated that 1,200 piezas should be delivered at that port annually. Of this number, 800 were to be sold to residents of the port city. The remainder were reserved for customers from the interior, who were expected to do their buying at the factory. However, the company soon learned that the demand in Buenos Aires was not enough to absorb 800 slaves year after year. Urged on by the factors, the court of directors approached the Spanish crown, outlined the problem, and requested permission to take the surplus slaves into the interior provinces and to Chile, Bolivia, and Peru. It tried to bolster its case by capitalizing on the well-known fear of slave rebellions, hinting that if its agents were restricted to Buenos Aires, "in a few years the number of slaves may be increased [at Buenos Aires] so as to endanger the town." Finally, the company would "be subject to risque of mortality, dieting, clothing and other damages" if the surplus slaves were not sold elsewhere.[30]

Overruling some of its officials, in 1725 the Spanish crown granted the company the right to sell surplus slaves in the interior, but with two important qualifications. The slaves could not be offered for sale in the "inland countries" within six months of their arrival at Buenos Aires. Nor could the slaves be sold until the company had obtained a legal document certifying that it had tried and failed to sell them in the city. The court of directors, far from pleased with this concession, bitterly denounced the terms as "being as bad as the disease." Keeping the slaves on hand for six months was intolerable; four to six weeks would be a reasonable delay.[31]

Even while the company negotiated with the Spanish, it was recommending that the factors connive with the colonial officers to disobey the restrictions. The court of directors hoped that its men had "cultivated so good a friendship with the men in power so as to get their leave or at least to wink at such of the negroes as are not vendible at Buenos Aires, going up as formerly, till the king of Spain's pleasure be further known." If friendship failed, a bribe might work. The court of directors delicately suggested that the factors would not "find it impossible by prudent management to procure some sort of certificate" to show that the slaves had spent the required time at Buenos Aires.[32]

To obtain the cooperation of the officials, the company instructed its employees to raise once again the specter of slave rebellions and epidemics should too many Africans be allowed to remain in Buenos Aires. "Such a conflux of negroes as this would in time produce," the court of directors predicted, "might infect the town with raging sickness, if not prove formidable and dangerous." If nothing else moved the Spaniards, they were to be reminded that the Portuguese stood ready to supply the "inland countrys" with illicit slaves "in detriment to the King of Spain's dutys"; the contraband trade would grievously damage "the town of Buenos Aires which receives so many advantages from our trade and shipping." The company was saddened at the thought that the townspeople would recognize the loss of their trade only "when too late."[33]

One may surmise that the Spanish officials found the offer of bribes a more persuasive reason for cooperation than dire predictions of rebellions, epidemics, or loss of trade. The Spanish crown seems never to have further liberalized its policy on the selling of slaves in the inland areas. But there is incontrovertible evidence that more and more slaves were sold outside of the port city as the years passed. Of course, it cannot be proved that all of these slaves did not remain in Buenos Aires for six months prior to being sent elsewhere, but it would be overcredulous to accept this proposition without reservations. It seems more likely that the officials were persuaded, whether by bribes or predictions of disaster, to ignore the violations of the king's order.

Although there was some variation in the size of the parties of slaves sent from Buenos Aires to Chile, Bolivia, or Peru, the average was from 100 to 400 in each group. These caravans were conducted by one or two Englishmen, several Spaniards, and perhaps some black slaves in the company's employ. A surgeon normally accompanied the party. The caravan, including the slaves, either traveled on foot or rode mules. The timing of the departure from Buenos Aires was crucial: if possible, the winter months were avoided because of the cold. Agent John Cox, for example, reported from Buenos Aires in 1731 that he had not sent any slaves to Potosí, the silver-mining town in upper Peru, in May because it was the "dead of winter." "Experienced men" had advised him that he would lose most of his cargo to the weather. The trek to Potosí seems to have been hazardous: of a caravan of 408 slaves (254 men and 154 women) dispatched there in 1731, thirty-eight men and twelve women died on the way and eleven men and nine women succumbed after reaching Potosí. This death rate of over 17 percent would have been high for the Atlantic passage in that period. Unfortunately, it cannot yet be determined whether this experience was typical for such inland journeys.[34]

Analysis of the records shows that at least 7,829 slaves were sold outside of Buenos Aires between 1715 and 1738, although not all were dispatched by the company's factors. Many of them, perhaps as high as 50 percent of the total, were carried by Spanish dealers who had bought them in large parcels at the factory for resale inland. In general, these slaves brought high prices in the "interior countrys," sometimes twice as much as in Buenos Aires. In a 1731 transaction at Potosí, a group of male slaves sold for 300 to 350 pesos each, at least 75 to 100 pesos more than a similar slave would have cost at the factory. Even more inflated, the price of females ranged between 480 and 550 pesos each, about twice their selling price at Buenos Aires. It is no wonder the company was so anxious to gain access to the interior markets.[35]

If, as one suspects, the Spanish officials at Buenos Aires accepted bribes from the English, their conduct was not at all unusual. The court of directors and the agents were aware that colonial officials and their superiors in Spain seldom refused "regalos" (gifts; a euphemism for bribes). A certain sum of money was specifically allocated each year to purchase the favors of the royal officials in Spain. In 1734 Benjamin Keene, the British ambassador, noted that he had been mandated by the company's late subgovernor and deputy governor "to dispose of as far as 500 pounds per annum to the ministers if I thought it would be for the Company's service." He had not yet spent the money, but he hoped the court of directors would approve "if at any time there shall be an occasion to make any small regalos." Keene thought that offering regalos was desirable and "well worth our while" to keep the Spanish officials "satisfied and to gain them to our interests."[36]

The situation was much the same in the colonies. Regalos were distributed at appropriate times, and small presents were offered to select officials on festive occasions, such as at Christmas. Nicholson and Tassell, agents at Havana between 1730 and 1734, disbursed 3,000 pesos in regalos during that time. They thought it only tactful "for strangers to support a friendly and obliging correspondence with people in power whereby to facilitate the exit of their concerns." They felt that value had been received for the money spent. Many lawsuits had been terminated in their favor, particularly those concerning the confiscation of illicitly introduced slaves. Slaves who arrived with smallpox had not been quarantined but were allowed to enter after a gratuity was offered to the officials in charge. Furthermore, the agents continued, they had been protected from "the dangerous intrusion of the ministers of the Inquisition." (Presumably the royal officials had persuaded the Inquisition to look the other way when confronted with some of the moral deficiencies of the Protestant English.)[37]

John Brown, a factor at Buenos Aires between 1731 and 1733, also admitted to spending money on "presents, wants and entertainment" for Spanish officials. But, unlike Nicholson and Tassell, he was far less convinced that the expenditures were always advantageous to the company. He gave the impression that such gifts were not voluntary but were really forced exactions; the "royal officers and all other ministers are sucking the English Asiento and Asientists' blood dearly." Brown's assertions, though harsh, had an element of truth. Regalos to officials had become a firmly established part of the trading process and were commonly given after a cargo of slaves had arrived, been examined, and allowed to land. Every crown employee who had been involved in any way in the clearance of a vessel expected a bribe: the chief royal official at the port (the English called him the governor), the accountant, the writer, and the lawyer. The amount of the regalo was suitable for the recipient's rank: governors averaged 200 pesos, and lesser officials 100 pesos each.[38]

Although the asiento contract committed the South Sea Company to meet the demand for slaves in all the Spanish American colonies, the court of directors recognized from the outset that the expense of establishing factories in small, remote, and thinly populated areas would be prohibitive. Still, the company was too jealous of the contraband traders to relinquish any part of the market to them; in addition, no one knew how the Spanish government might react if the company failed to fulfill its part of the contract. The court of directors solved the problem by selling licenses to selected individuals to do small-scale trading in certain areas.

The company started the license system two years after accepting the asiento. On October 17, 1716, the court of directors announced, rather prematurely, that it was "inclined" to receive the traders' proposals "for licensing their negro trade as may be advantageous to the Company." Eventually the company decided that the Windward Coast (defined broadly as Caracas, Margarita, Santa Marta, Río de la Hacha, Trinidad, Maracaibo, Santo Domingo, Puerto Rico, and the coast between Nicaragua and Campeche) would be supplied with slaves through the licensed trade.[39]

After deliberation the company agreed to share the responsibility for granting licenses with Dudley Woodbridge, its chief agent at Barbados. The same authority was later extended to the Jamaica agents. Woodbridge was empowered on January 9, 1717, to grant two types of licenses: an authorization to bring slaves into a designated colony and receive payment in cash, or an authorization that allowed the licensee to accept payment in goods ("fruits of the country"). A license was good for one voyage, and the vessel had to carry the company's coat of arms. The slaves were to be branded with the company's seal to minimize the risk of illicit trade. If the trader employed black sailors, the licensing agent had to record their names and make sure they returned with the ship. Licensees who paid the company before the voyage would receive a discount of 2.5 percent; those who chose time payments would be charged interest at the rate of 10 percent per annum. Finally, a licensee who failed to sell all of his slaves could sell the remainder at a company factory at the rate of 125 pesos per pieza.[40]

Woodbridge seems not to have issued many licenses, probably because the company was slow to decide what to charge for them. During a visit to England in October, 1717, he recommended a charge of 80 or 100 pesos per pieza for slaves brought to the Windward Coast.[41] All licensed traders, Woodbridge suggested, should be encouraged to take payment in cocoa, which could then be sold at any company factory. In this way, he argued, "the planters will be enabled to purchase the more negroes, but without it no more can be sold than can be paid for in cash which is very scarce in those parts and the profit the licensed persons will have by the cocoa will encourage and enable them to give the more for the license and carry on that trade to the greatest extent." Since the cocoa trade was generally thought to be profitable, Woodbridge proposed that those who engaged in it should pay 100 pesos per pieza; the others would pay the 80-peso rate. Only traders who bought a license for ten or more piezas would be eligible for the cocoa terms. All slaves were to be branded before departure; the licensee would be fined £100 for each unmarked slave. Woodbridge also proposed that licenses could be sold for an extended period, not just for one voyage. These proposals were endorsed by the company, and Woodbridge was authorized "to farm the sole trade to the Windward Coast as far as Río de La Hacha inclusive to any person or persons for a certain term not exceeding 3 years."[42]

Several private traders wanted to negotiate for a license. The factors at Barbados and later at Jamaica received proposals from men who wanted to have the trade farmed out to them for a number of years. Other proposals went directly to the court of directors in England. An early proposal came from Antonio Francisco de Coulange in September, 1717; he planned to purchase slaves at St. Thomas, a Danish-owned island, for 104 pesos per head and resell twenty of them annually at Puerto Rico at 250 pesos each. He expected to realize a profit of 2,000 pesos a year and would be satisfied with 500 pesos as his share. A committee considered his proposal, but there is no evidence that the license was ever awarded.[43]

The company received at least two other proposals in 1717. The Sieur Durepaire made a vague request to farm Puerto Rico and Santo Domingo and to supply some additional slaves to Caracas, Santa Marta, and Cartagena. Since his proposal lacked such basic information as the number of slaves he expected to deliver and dates of delivery, he was asked to resubmit it in greater detail. There is no evidence that he ever did so. Another proposal came from Lewis Renard of Amsterdam. A company committee opened serious discussions with Renard for supplying 400 slaves (240 men between twenty and twenty-five, eighty women between sixteen and twenty, forty boys age ten to fifteen, and forty girls age twelve to fifteen), "the women as near as possible [to] be all virgins." Renard and the committee could not agree, and his proposal was shelved.[44]

If these cases are any indication, the company carefully scrutinized each proposal before granting a license. The company had to be convinced that the proposal was feasible, that the applicant could execute it, and that he would not engage in contraband trade. Normally, a proposal had to include a detailed statement of the expected expenditures and profits. A statement submitted by William Lea in 1736 shows the care with which these documents were prepared (see Table 5). Lea wanted to supply 200 slaves to Guatemala (134 piezas) in return for 10 percent of the profits. After outlining the projected costs of the slaves and their clothing, food, medical care, transportation, and so on, Lea calculated the company's profit at £827 19s.[45]

Another proposal in 1736 came from Neil Bothwell, who wanted a license to trade with Santo Domingo. Bothwell proposed to introduce 125 slaves into that island in return for 6.5 percent of the profits. He guaranteed the company a profit of £1,106 10s. annually. His proposal was not as detailed as Lea's, but it served the purpose (see Table 6).

The loss of the bulk of the company's financial records makes it impossible to determine the number of licenses granted. Certainly, a number of proposals were approved, although it seems, at least in the first few years, that there were fewer applicants than the company would have liked. On July 13, 1718, the court of directors expressed disappointment that only four licenses had been awarded for a total of ninety-three slaves, and urged Woodbridge "to improve this opportunity all you can." In 1723 Richard Harris received three licenses to deliver thirty slaves to Puerto Rico, for which he was to pay the company 80 pesos per slave. Two partners, Collett and Perrie, also received several licenses in 1729 and 1730 to take slaves to various places on the Windward Coast, and Blackwood and

TABLE 5. Lea's Estimate for Trade to Guatemala, 1736

Debit	Pesos	£ s. d.
To first cost of 200 negroes at £18 each		3,600 0. 0.
King of Spain's duty at 134 piezas being mostly children at 33⅓ pesos	4,446⅔	1,002 10. 0.
Clothing etc. at Jamaica before shipping at 3 pesos each	600	135 0. 0.
Duty at Jamaica on exportation at 20s. per head		133 6. 0.
Sloop hire and wages at £100 per month for 10 months		1,000 0. 0.
Provisions for sailors at 2 pesos per diem for 30 days	600	135 0. 0.
Mortality on negroes at 5 percent [7 percent?]		252 0. 0.
Maintenance of 5 negro servants	228	51 6. 0.
Maintenance of 200 negroes for 182 days at ⅔ real per day		549 18. 0.
Salary to Judge Conservator	1,500	337 10. 0.
Salary to lawyer, solicitor and scrivener	600	135 0. 0.
Physick and nursing slaves at 3 pesos per head	600	135 0. 0.
Warehouse rent at River Dulcea [and] Regalos to Castellanos, other officers and soldiers	500	112 10. 0.
Mule hire from thence to Guatemala	800	180 0. 0.
Rent of a house and warehouse at Guatemala	800	180 0. 0.
House keeping per annum 2,000 [pesos] Bookkeeper's wages 400 One white servant's wages 100 Clothing him and two negroes in liveries 150	2,650	596 5. 0.
Contingency's per annum	350	78 15. 0.
Sloops register and clearance etc. for 2 voyages	600	135 0. 0.
Commission at 10 percent to factor		1,000 0. 0.
		£9,749 0. 0.
Gain to South Sea Company		£ 827 19. 0.
		£10,577 0. 0.
		[£10,576 19. 0.]
For sale of 200 negroes at 235 pesos per head	47,000	10,577 0. 0.

SOURCE: Shelburne MSS, vol. 43, 258–59.

TABLE 6. Bothwell's Estimate for Trade to Santo Domingo, 1736

Debit	£ s. d.
To cost of 125 slaves at £20	2,500 0. 0.
To commission at 5%	125 0. 0.
To sloop hire	500 0. 0.
To salary of Judge Conservator	450 0. 0.
To the Secretary and other officers	450 0. 0.
To house rent	90 0. 0.
To housekeeping and maintaining the negroes unsold	450 0. 0.
To servants' wages	67 10. 0.
To Bothwell's commission at 6½%	381 0. 0.
Total	£4,833 10. 0.

Credit	£ s. d.
Sale of 120 negroes at 220 pesos each	5,940 0. 0.
To 5 negroes supposed to die	
Total	£5,940 0. 0.
Annual profit £5,940 0. 0. − £4,833 10s. =	£1,106 10. 0.

SOURCE: Shelburne MSS, vol. 43, 210–11.

Cathcart were licensed to introduce 199 slaves into Campeche between 1730 and 1733.[46]

An analysis of the company's shipping records for the period January, 1731, to December, 1733, shows a surprising volume of licensed trade during these thirty-six months. Of 109 vessels carrying slaves from Jamaica to Spanish America, 41 (38 percent) were licensed. As Table 7 shows, these 109 ships carried a total of 12,193 slaves. The licensed vessels transported 2,344 (19.25 percent), quite a high proportion. In other words, about one out of every five slaves delivered during those three years was not carried in a company ship. There is no reason to assume that these years were in any way atypical of the period. Evidently the licensed traders played a crucial supporting role in the conduct of the asiento trade. It is also noteworthy that they virtually monopolized the smaller markets where the company did not settle, while the company's own vessels were always sent to the factories at the larger ports.

Not all the licensees realized a profit; several traders met with bad markets and were either forced to dispose of their slaves very cheaply or had to sell them at one of the company factories for the low price of 125

TABLE 7. Slaves Carried on Licensed and Company Ships, 1731–33

Destination	Number of Company Ships	Number of Licensed Ships	Number of Slaves on Company Ships	Number of Slaves on Licensed Ships
Maracaibo		3		139
Puerto Rico		6		115
Caracas		18		1,658
Santo Domingo		3		103
Campeche		9		167
Guatemala		2		162
Cartagena	16		2,625	
Havana	20		1,832	
Porto Bello	18		4,538	
Santiago de Cuba	9		520	
Vera Cruz	5		334	
Total	68	41	9,849	2,344

SOURCE: AGI, Contaduría 267, ramo 8.

pesos each. Others suffered losses from high mortality or ran into costly delays in their voyages. William Ramsey lost money on his voyages to several parts of the Windward Coast in 1717 and to Trinidad in 1727. Messrs. Collett and Perrie reported in 1729 that their losses on the Windward Coast were extensive. In 1733 "sundry gentlemen" in Jamaica wrote the company that they had had a miserable time in introducing seventy-six slaves into Guatemala. Some of their slaves died of smallpox and many more were unfit for sale. The market was poor. These difficulties may not have been typical, but they were certainly not unique.[47]

Several unlucky or incompetent licensees applied to the company for financial relief. In 1717, for example, Nathaniel White, licensed to introduce 140 slaves at Caracas, failed to sell all of them there and was forced to dispose of the remainder at the factory at Havana. White's eight- or nine-week project turned into a nine-month nightmare. He estimated his loss on the license at £300. The court of directors was moderately sympathetic and gave him £100.[48]

At least two licensees betrayed the company. In 1718 Jonathan Sisson and Thomas Ottley jointly received a license to introduce some slaves into Caracas, Santo Domingo, and Puerto Rico. Without the company's knowledge the two men established factories in the company's name at Caracas and Puerto Rico and installed their own agents. Furthermore, they with-held payment for their license and continued to introduce slaves long after it had expired. When their duplicity was eventually discovered, the com-pany appealed to the Spanish officials to impound their possessions. The Spaniards, doubtless bribed by Sisson and Ottley, gave the company pre-cious little satisfaction. The court of directors charged that the governor of Puerto Rico "seems resolved to favour the interest of these impos-tors rather than the Company." Many years later, in 1731, the company brought suit against Sisson, who admitted that he owed £11,551 7s. for his license but insisted that he could not pay the debt, since much of his property had been seized by the Spaniards during the war of 1727–29. Sisson agreed to give the company a bond for £2,009 15s., payable before May 1, 1733, and to sign over his remaining assets in Spanish America, valued at 38,248 pesos (£8,605). Whether the company recovered its money is not known.[49]

The license trade came to an abrupt halt in 1733 when Spain decided to disallow it. The crown discovered rather belatedly that the asiento con-tract had not sanctioned the farming out of the trade. The change in policy was merely one symptom of the general disaffection brought about by dis-putes over other matters. The Spanish turned a deaf ear to the company's argument that the illicit traders who paid no duty would take over the business that the licensees had handled.[50]

The court of directors was hopeful of reaching an accommodation with the Spaniards on licensing. In 1735 it even invited new proposals for licenses, and in the following year the company evaluated two of them favorably, including one from William Lea. Nothing came of these or any other licensing plans; the Spanish government remained obdurate.[51] The impasse with the Spaniards was never overcome, and the War of Jenkins' Ear terminated the discussion permanently.

The asiento trade, as has been seen, was beset with difficulties. It sel-dom functioned smoothly and was interrupted at least twice by war be-tween Spain and England. The planters in Jamaica resented the South Sea Company's presence, and the Assembly's harassment was a constant irri-tant. For their part, the interlopers made unconvincing and exaggerated complaints about their exclusion from the Spanish market. The license trade helped to ensure that the smaller markets were not ignored, but over-all the supply of slaves was unpredictable at best. Not surprisingly, the Spaniards were unhappy with the company's conduct of the asiento and traded openly and consistently with the contraband traders.

NOTES

1. BM, 25576, p. 121.

2. The new policy paid the agents at the larger factories a commission on the sale of the slaves which varied between 4 and 5 percent. In addition, they received 2.5 percent of the value of the "returns," such as silver, hides, and cocoa, which they sent to England or to Jamaica in the ships. There was also a fixed allowance to cover the maintenance cost of each slave until he was sold. Since the gross value of the business conducted at Vera Cruz was less than at the other factories, the agents there received 5 percent commission on both sales and returns. In 1734 the commission on returns at Vera Cruz was increased to 6 percent. See BM, 25564, pp. 104–11; 25576, pp. 76–87.

3. BM, 25551, pp. 52–53; 25550, p. 53. For conversion purposes, 1 peso = 4s. 6d. (sterling).

4. Ibid.

5. During the 1730s the company reduced the allocation for maintenance at Barbados to 5d. a day. Throughout the period the Barbadian and Jamaican pounds were valued at about 30–40 percent less than the pound sterling. Unless otherwise noted, the calculations in this study are made in pounds sterling.

6. BM, 25555, p. 78.

7. BM, 25557, p. 61; Shelburne MSS, vol. 44, 817.

8. AGI, Indiferente, 2847. A "refuse negro" sold in Jamaica was subject to the payment of a tax of 10s. in Jamaica and 5s. in Barbados.

9. PRO, T70/52, p. 15.

10. See the instructions to the Captains in BM, 25567; Shelburne MSS, vol. 44, 896, 595.

11. PRO, T70/51, p. 82; T70/52, p. 15; Shelburne MSS, vol. 44, 595.

12. Some Observations on the Assiento Trade as It Has Been Exercised by the South Sea Company . . . by a Person Who Resided Several Years at Jamaica, 2d ed. (London, 1728), p. 4; BM, 25561, pp. 27–36; 25564, pp. 104–11.

13. BM, 25564, p. 13.

14. Shelburne MSS, vol. 43, 127; AGI, Contaduría 267, ramos 1–6; AGI, Indiferente, 2847. These charges seem to have been based on Barbadian and Jamaican currency rather than on pounds sterling.

15. CO, vol. 137, no. 12, pt. 2, 311.

16. CO, vol. 137, no. 12, pt. 1, 35.

17. Some Observations on the Assiento Trade, p. 20; CSP, no. 245 (1732), p. 129.

18. BM, 25559, p. 49.

19. BM, 25555, p. 77.

20. BM, 25561, pp. 28–36.

21. BM, 25556, p. 54; CO, vol. 137, 279–80.

22. BM, 25561, pp. 28–36.

23. Ibid., 25507, pp. 101–2.

24. BM, 25563, p. 82; 25503, p. 69.

25. CSP, no. 328 (1732), pp. 187–88.

26. BM, 25561, pp. 27–36.

27. BM, 25575, p. 15.

28. BM, 25565, pp. 65–73.

29. AGI, Indiferente, 2805.

30. BM, 25564, pp. 86–91, 97.

31. BM, 25553, pp. 13–27.

32. BM, 25565, pp. 67–75.

33. Ibid.

34. Shelburne MSS, vol. 44, 395.

35. Elena F. S. de Studer, *La trata de negros en el Río de la Plata durante el siglo XVIII* (Buenos Aires: Departamento Editorial, Universidad de Buenos Aires, 1958), p. 236; AGI, Audiencia de Buenos Aires, vol. 591. It is not clear why women commanded such high prices in Potosí. Possibly this was due to their childbearing potential or to the great demand for female domestic slaves. Transportation costs to the "inland countrys" helped to account for the high prices of both males and females.

36. BM, 32783, p. 381.

37. Shelburne MSS, vol. 43, 155.

38. Shelburne MSS, vol. 44, 144.

39. BM, 25496, p. 165.

40. BM, 25563, pp. 116–22.

41. Woodbridge suggested that two or three children under six should count as one pieza, three boys between six and sixteen two piezas, and three girls between six and twelve or thirteen two piezas. All males over sixteen and girls over twelve or thirteen should count as one pieza. See BM, 25550, pp. 88, 93.

42. BM, 25550, p. 93. It is not clear whether the fine was to be paid in pounds sterling or in Barbadian currency.

43. BM, 25550, p. 82.

44. BM, 25550, pp. 83, 94–95.

45. Note some oddities in the table. Lea assumes a 5 percent mortality, but his calculation seems actually to be based on 7 percent. He then makes no allowance for deaths when he calculates his credits; he expected to sell all 200 slaves.

46. BM, 25563, p. 201; 25557, pp. 76–77; 25553, pp. 10–11; Shelburne MSS, vol. 43, 267.

47. BM, 25553, pp. 1, 10–11; 25550, p. 98; 25506, p. 269.

48. BM, 25550, p. 98. Payment was made in Barbadian currency.

49. BM, 25576, pp. 8–9; 25564, p. 63.

50. BM, 32782, p. 303.

51. BM, 25505, pp. 203–4; 25545, pp. 57, 18, 61; 25554, p. 4; 25507, p. 179.

5 The Illegal Slave Trade

From the days of Queen Elizabeth I the English had delighted in defying the Spanish imperial system by encouraging a fairly extensive contraband trade in slaves and other commodities with the Spanish colonies. The market for slaves, flour, woolens and other textiles, and various manufactured articles was sometimes brisk. Spain could not meet these mercantile demands, and the asiento system allowed the colonists to trade with the contracting nation only under crippling restrictions, especially for goods other than slaves. Moreover, the asentista's monopoly put him in a position to set his own prices, which were usually high enough to drive potential customers into the arms of the contraband traders.

The Spanish colonial officials found it convenient and lucrative to cooperate with the interlopers, and some even engaged in the illegal trade themselves. English officials were pleased at the Spanish crown's demonstrated inability to enforce the law in its own empire. The Spaniards chafed under the loss of much-needed tax revenue, and they fulminated against the contraband trade because it drained an unknown but ever-increasing quantity of bullion from the empire into foreign hands. As long as these foreign hands were English, Whitehall was pleased with the situation.

There can be no doubt that the Royal African Company began to carry on contraband trade with the Spaniards shortly after it was chartered in 1672. The South Sea Company, however, was not tempted to engage in the illegal trade, probably because it never had slaves left over after its annual contractual obligations were fulfilled. But for the company, every contraband slave sold to the Spaniards represented a reduction in its own profits. Understandably, it wanted to ensure that its employees, particularly the captains of its slave ships, would not smuggle slaves for their personal gain.

In an attempt to stamp out illicit trading on the part of its captains, the South Sea Company forbade them to purchase any slaves in Africa on their private account. Captains who received permission to make private purchases of African commodities for resale promised to deal only in gold, redwood, and ivory. Predictably, the restrictions were not always obeyed, but some captains who had violated their pledge voluntarily confessed their wrongdoing to the company. For example, in 1729 Captain Webb of the *Wootle* reported that he had purchased thirty-four slaves with his "private adventure"; four had died, but thirty had been delivered at Buenos Aires and the company could buy them at an appropriate price. The court of directors agreed to pay Webb £20 per head but fined him £50 for violating his charter. Later that year another captain made a similar report; in this case the company paid him £390 for his twenty-two slaves and repeated its prohibition against private trade in slaves.[1]

In 1730 some captains petitioned the company to abrogate the ban on private trade in slaves, since there was "no gold and seldom any elephants teeth [ivory] at Angola where they are bound." The court of directors agreed that the request was reasonable, but to grant it would legitimize participation in the slave trade by all the captains and might even encourage them to engage in the contraband trade as well. In lieu of liberalizing its policy, the court of directors promised the captains "a further gratuity over and above the commission allowed by charter-party." Such concessions evidently did not accomplish their purpose; as late as 1733 Thomas Geraldino, the Spanish agent in London, accused the "agents, factors and masters of vessels" employed by the company of "abusing the confidence and sincerity which they ought to have practiced" by "carrying on an illicit trade."[2]

The illicit private traders of British nationality fitted out their vessels in one of the islands, such as Barbados or Jamaica. They kept no records, so it is impossible to calculate the number of slaves they sold to the Spaniards. There are indications, however, that the trade was considerable and that it was increasing during the years when the South Sea Company held the asiento.

Even the crews aboard the English men-of-war that patrolled the seas engaged in illicit trade. As early as June, 1714, the factors at Cartagena asked to have these ships prohibited from "carrying negroes to the Spanish coast on any account whatsoever." The South Sea Company confessed in 1723 that it was powerless to stop the navy's trade in contraband slaves. It replied to the complaints of the agents at Porto Bello, "As to what you write concerning our men of war protecting and carrying on the private trade, we are not insensible, however beneficial it may be to the Nation in general, it is a great damage to the Company in particular, but as it is not within our province to complain of it, you must be the more diligent in seizing the negroes on their arrival."[3]

French, Portuguese, and Dutch slavers also traded illegally with the Spanish colonies. The French, who held the asiento between 1702 and 1713, continued the trade despite the Treaty of Utrecht. In fact, the South Sea Company complained in 1714 that there were at least twenty-seven French ships in the colonies "which must lessen the navigation of Great Britain. . . . The French lower the prices of goods and carry the riches of the whole Indies into their dominions." In response to the company's protests, the French blandly claimed that the Guinea Company had the rights to continue trading with the Spaniards for three years after the expiration of their asiento contract. The Spaniards repudiated the French claim; article 18 of the asiento contract with the English expressly forbade the French Guinea Company to introduce slaves into Spanish America after May 1, 1713. A royal cédula of April 15, 1713, repeated the prohibition. Finally, the king of Spain's cédula of May 15, 1718, required all French traders to leave the colonies.[4]

It is doubtful whether the French ever completely abandoned commerce with Spanish America. The company's records reveal that between May 1, 1713, and December, 1717, French traders introduced 588 slaves into the port of Havana. By 1719 they had also brought 229 slaves to Porto Bello and 213 to Cartagena. Further evidence of continued French activity appears in a letter sent from Loango in 1724 by Captain Williams of the *Syrria*. He wrote, "The French have a great trade to this coast," adding that two French sailors confessed that they sold all their slaves to the Spaniards at Santo Domingo "and that they have guarda la costas cruising there to protect their trade."[5]

The Portuguese were also active in the illicit slave trade, particularly in Buenos Aires and Peru. The court of directors of the South Sea Company even hinted at connivance between the Portuguese and the factors at Buenos Aires. A group of thirty-seven slaves near Lima in 1723 was found to lack the company's "mark," although the certificate stated that the group had been dispatched from Buenos Aires. The asiento contract forbade the company to send slaves from Buenos Aires to Lima. Hence the court of directors suspected that the slaves belonged to Portuguese interlopers who had obtained a company certificate from the agents at Buenos

Aires. The agents denied the accusation, and the court of directors confessed that the incident "was really such a mystery that if we had not a good opinion of your probity [it] might give us room to suspect some underhand dealings between you, or some of you and the Portuguese." Based on extant evidence, collusion between the Portuguese and the factors cannot be established; suffice it to say that many Englishmen were not noted for fidelity to the honest conduct of their employer's affairs.[6]

Spanish officials closed their eyes to Portuguese infractions of the asiento. Captain Goldsborough, a visitor at the Buenos Aires factory in 1731, reported that "it was impossible to sell 50 negroes in 6 months" at Buenos Aires because the Portuguese "bring more than the place can take off." He added that the royal officials condoned the contraband trade. His estimate of the position was too pessimistic, but the Portuguese were definitely a nuisance to the company's trade at Buenos Aires. As late as 1735 the South Sea Company was still complaining about the introduction of slaves into Buenos Aires from Brazil and asking for more effective enforcement of the law. Later that year royal officials apprehended and confiscated a number of those slaves.[7]

Unlike the French and Portuguese, the Dutch had never held the asiento contract. Dutch traders, however, were quite successful in building up a thriving slave trade with the Spaniards from their bases on the islands of Curaçao and St. Eustatius. Some Dutch vessels were occasionally intercepted by the Spaniards and the slaves confiscated, but such instances were exceptional.[8]

The court of directors realized that a flourishing contraband trade would adversely affect the company's financial health. The illegal traders did not have to support factories and they paid no duty. Thus their overhead was lower than the company's, and they could afford to undercut prices. Competition sometimes forced the company, against its better judgment, to reduce prices. In 1734, for example, the company's committee of correspondence agreed that to prevent the illicit introduction of slaves into Cuba "and to encourage the sales for the Company's account, the factors be directed to lower the price to 200 pesos [£40] per head."[9]

Understandably, the company was disturbed by the extent of the illegal slave trade. From a very early date the court of directors had urged vigilance in reporting illegal traders to the local authorities. In 1717 the men at Vera Cruz were admonished to "use your best endeavours to prevent smuggling in goods and slaves." Article 18 of the asiento contract gave the English the right to confiscate illicit cargoes of slaves, a right that the company often urged its people to exercise. In 1716 the court of directors asked its agents in Jamaica (a major center for the dispatch of contraband slaves) to let the factors "know of any design for clandestine voyages so such may be seized upon arrival." And in 1723 it urged the Buenos Aires agents to "put into operation the power you have to seize."[10]

The South Sea Company was convinced that a vigorous and sustained campaign to seize illicit slaves was the best deterrent to the contraband trade. But the seizure of cargoes could be hazardous; irate owners threatened and even assaulted the men who were about to seize their property. The company complained in 1718 that the factors at Havana had been "obstructed in their endeavours" to stop the contraband trade. When the factors there authorized "a person of the best estate and fairest character" to seize contraband slaves at Puerto del Príncipe, he "was prevented from putting the same into execution, the populace at Puerto Príncipe threatening that if he offered to seize a negro or disturb the private traders they would hang him and his power on the highest tree." In July, 1728, the court of directors examined "the abuses and violences committed on the person of Don Juan Labadie when he was endeavoring to seize illicit negroes, he having been employed by the Panama and Porto Bello factory." It also took note of the "other proofs of obstructions given by the Spaniards to the factors or those employed by them in seizing illicit negroes."[11]

In 1731 agents Dennis and Cocke at Havana feared for their safety if they tried to seize slaves illicitly introduced into Cuba. Although Havana "and indeed all the country round is full of illicit negroes," they said, it would be "next to madness to attempt to seize them ourselves." Two years later the two agents declined to move against illicit slaves at Puerto del Príncipe and Bayamo in Cuba because "the inhabitants live, as it were, exempt of Spain's government, having no garrison or governor among them . . . and as those people are very numerous and all alike guilty, their numbers protect them against any attempt to seize either their illicit negroes or goods." Undoubtedly, the possibility of reprisals deterred some agents from pursuing an aggressive policy.[12]

Seizing a cargo was sometimes easier than keeping it in custody. In a letter to the factors at Panama in 1723, the company mentioned "the violent rescue of the 44 negroes . . . and also the other rescue of negroes committed by the Viceking . . . being the cause of over 400 more escaping." Two years later the company complained of "the violent rescues of the negroes our people had seized" in Peru.[13]

The illegal trade could not have flourished without the collaboration of the royal officials. The South Sea Company frequently denounced the local bureaucrats for venality and corruption. Writing in 1716 to George Bubb, the English envoy at Madrid, the court of directors protested that "the introduction of great quantities of negroes . . . is winked at by persons in power there [the colonies] . . . [and] seems to be authorized by them." Furthermore, the agents at Porto Bello maintained that 3,000 slaves had been introduced there illegally since the asiento contract began "and that the royal officers have set a mark upon them to enable them to pass more easily in the country as if they had been legally imported." Two years later the company alleged that the chief royal officer at Panama had accepted a bribe of 2,500 pesos (£500) from an illegal trader to ignore charges that he had transported and sold slaves in Peru.[14]

Whether the many specific charges of venality were true, the company certainly believed them. In 1729 the court of directors badgered Ambassador Keene at Madrid to protest "the encouragement given by the Spanish officers to clandestine introductions of negroes, particularly in the island of Cuba and Cartagena." An official report prepared in 1739 proved what nobody doubted, that "a considerable private trade" from Jamaica "is wink'd at by the Governors and royal officers who as it is said generally buy their cargoes by persons they appoint for that purpose. The Merchants' private trade is carried on by sloops, who do not go into their harbours, but not far from them on the coast of Cartagena and Porto Bello chiefly, where the Spaniards come off to them in canoes or other boats which bring their money and carry their goods ashore."[15]

Given no satisfaction by the Spaniards, the company fell back on blaming its factors for the growth of the contraband trade. After noting that the "private traders sell their negroes almost without fear of seizure from you," the court of directors lambasted the agents at Porto Bello in 1723 for their "indulgence and want of activity" in ferreting out such traders. The following year it blamed the "remissness" of the factors in Cuba for the continuation of the illicit trade in that island.[16]

The company's suspicion that its employees were actively involved in the contraband trade was not unfounded. In 1738 an agent at Buenos Aires uncovered evidence that two of his predecessors had been active in the illicit trade. The agents in Jamaica and Barbados who dispatched both slave ships and provision ships conspired on occasion with the captains and crews to conceal some of the cargo from the Spanish officials. Quite a few provision ships also carried slaves to be sold clandestinely to the Spaniards. Some slave ships tried to evade payment of the duty on slaves by hiding part of their cargo. However, the number of company ships on which contraband slaves were found was far less than the number of ships trying to smuggle flour, textiles, and other consumer goods.[17]

Normally the South Sea Company insisted that its factors refuse to buy slaves from the contraband traders even at attractive prices. Apart from the question of unseemliness, such deals would encourage the interlopers to continue to infringe upon the company's monopoly. In 1716 the factors at Vera Cruz bought seventy-three slaves at 120 pesos (£24) per head from a private trader who was intercepted but insisted that he was en route to the Carolinas in North America. The court of directors censured the purchase; the slaves should have been confiscated in accordance with the terms of the asiento contract, since such purchases provide "an encouragement to carry on that illicit trade to the detriment of our own." When the factors at Porto Bello in 1723 suggested that the company do business with these outsiders, the company damned the idea as "absurd" and "gross," adding that "it deserved no answer but a flat denial." The court of directors feared that any dealings with private traders would contribute to their proliferation and that they "would in time become almost the sole importers as well of goods as negroes."[18]

Nevertheless, on at least one occasion the company approved of doing business with a private trader. In February, 1717, the Havana agents purchased 129 slaves from a Mr. Wood. The court of directors endorsed this exception to its policy because the transaction occurred "at a juncture when the people were so mutinous even to rise up against the king of Spain's officers." Of course, clearing a profit of £3,088 on the deal helped overcome any hesitation the company might have felt.[19]

When Spanish officials seized contraband Africans (called "prize" slaves), the asiento contract required that such slaves be handed over to the company to be sold. In return, the company had to pay the officials a suitable reward. A royal cédula of 1717 set a price of 118 pesos for each pieza de Indias taken as a prize and turned over to the company. Prize slaves were subject to the usual duty and were considered part of the annual total that the company was obligated to deliver.[20]

Although the royal officials duly relinquished to the company the majority of prize slaves, sometimes they sold the slaves and kept the proceeds. In one case, reported in 1717, officials seized 170 slaves aboard a Jamaican sloop off Cartagena and sold them for 100 or more pesos each. Again, in 1725 the agents at Jamaica complained that the officials at Campeche had sold some prize slaves but refused to turn over the proceeds to the company. Finally, in 1737 the officials at Cartagena sold sixteen prize slaves and kept the money.[21]

The company continued to protest against these infractions of the contract. In 1725 the Spanish crown issued a cédula ordering that the proceeds from all prize slaves seized since May 1, 1713, be turned over to the company. This command was no more effective than any other concerning illicit trade. Despairing of Spanish law enforcement, the South Sea Company in 1735 appealed to the British crown, but to no avail. The prize slave imbroglio continued to embitter relations between the company and Spain until the end of the asiento contract.[22]

The company's records and Spanish documents provide only patchy data on the number of prize slaves that were seized. The records are fairly complete for the years 1716 to 1719, when 231 slaves were seized at Porto Bello and Panama, 199 at Cartagena, 40 at Vera Cruz, and 91 at Havana. Thereafter, fragmentary data show that at least twenty-eight slaves were seized at Cartagena between 1722 and 1737, forty-six at Porto Bello and Panama between 1722 and 1735, and forty-three at Vera Cruz between 1733 and 1737.[23]

Since seizure was a risky operation and not particularly effective in destroying the contraband trade, the company resorted to the use of the "indulto." This device legalized illicit slave purchases retroactively with the penalty of a fine. An indulto was offered in a particular district, and there were two types, limited and general. A limited indulto applied only to slaves purchased during a specified time period, whereas the general indulto included all illicit slaves, regardless of when they were bought.

The company proposed the conditions of the indulto, but only the issuance of a promulgation, or bando, by the royal officials could officially open it. Usually the owners of illicit slaves were given ten to fourteen days in which to "manifest" them (i.e., bring them to the officials in charge of the indulto and pay a fine). The indulto fine varied with the colony and with whether the slave was judged to be a pieza. After the fine was paid, the slave was branded with the company's "mark" and was no longer liable to seizure. Each indulted slave was credited to the company's account and subject to payment of the duty as stipulated in the asiento contract. It was therefore important that the company set the indulto fine high enough to cover the duty and yield a profit, but not so high as to discourage owners from "manifesting" their illicit slaves.

Prior to 1723 the court of directors of the South Sea Company let its agents set the amount of the fine and choose the time and place to indult the slaves. Later the company wondered about the wisdom and honesty of its employees and questioned the low fines they were setting. Consequently, in 1723 the court of directors assumed the power of determining when and where an indulto would be opened as well as setting the amount of the fine.

Throughout the period the fine for each pieza ranged between 50 and 100 pesos (£10 and £20). In areas like Puerto Rico, Santo Domingo, and some parts of Cuba where the residents were poor and the demand for slaves low, the indulto was normally fixed at 50 pesos per pieza. Since 33⅓ pesos had to be paid the crown as duty, such low fines cut into the profit margin. The agents would then try to negotiate with the local officials to pay only a portion of the duty.[24]

The residents of the more wealthy and populous areas of the empire, such as Panama and Cartagena, had to pay an indulto fine of 80 or 100 pesos on each pieza. To those sections—such as Campeche, Río de la Hacha, Maracaibo, Cumaná—where the company did not have factories, a special agent would be sent to open an indulto. These agents received a commission on each pieza that was "manifested," which drove the price still higher. The fine for those areas seems to have remained at 100 pesos per pieza throughout the period.[25]

Some indultos were relatively successful. The one held at Porto Bello in 1723 brought forth 389 slaves; at Santiago de Cuba in 1733 the owners paid fines on 145 illicit slaves. Other indultos, however, failed miserably. One that opened in Lima in 1718 was largely ignored, prompting the agents to initiate a vigorous campaign of seizures of "such as don't come in." The residents of Puerto del Príncipe explained away an indulto fiasco in 1733 by claiming to be too poor.[26]

Indultos created some problems of their own. The company usually set its slave prices between 200 and 300 pesos, but the interlopers sold contraband slaves for 120 pesos or less. A shrewd customer might buy the cheap illicit slave, legalize him for 100 pesos or less at an indulto, and save himself money. Thus an indulto especially with a low fine, could actually stimulate the illegal trade. There is even some evidence that after a number of Spaniards had their slaves indulted, they resold them at a profit, either locally or in another colony. In 1731 agents Cocke and Dennis at Santiago de Cuba accused the islanders of wanting an indulto so "they can send the negroes they now have to Havana, Cartagena and Porto Bello and sell them there at Asiento prices and with the returns purchase two or three for one they now have." Two years later agents Nicholson and Tassell at

Havana opposed a new indulto because "any indulgence of that kind to the illegal traders will animate them to provide themselves with fresh quantities in hopes of the like occasion of indult happening. . . . The people can buy slaves cheaply on the coast or in the inland country, three for the value of one here and by indulting them, save nearly half what they would cost if bought from us."[27]

The company was acutely conscious of the abuses arising out of the indulto. This awareness led the court of directors in 1723 to assume the full responsibility for opening indultos. The letter that informed the factors at Buenos Aires not to undertake any more indultos on their own volition also reprimanded the factors for setting the fine of a previous indulto at only 60 pesos per pieza. Later that year the agents at Porto Bello were rebuked for opening a general indulto, since that practice was "encouraging to the private and destructive to our own trade." The agents had justified the indulto in question as being the precursor to a campaign to confiscate illicit slaves, a notion that was rejected as "fallacious." The court of directors was especially incensed to hear that the fine was set at only 80 pesos per pieza; the angry letter accused the factors of complicity with the interlopers, charging that the indulto "was calculated to favour the private traders and yourselves."[28]

No evidence substantiates these charges of corruption leveled against the Porto Bello factors. In any event, the company could not have obtained supporting documentation unless one of its men in Porto Bello gave evidence against his fellows, and none was ever forthcoming. The only practical effect of this affair was that the factors lost the right to initiate indultos. Owing to this and other instances of factor-initiated indultos, the court of directors became firmly convinced that the seizure of slaves was a better way of dealing with the contraband problem. A confiscated slave could be sold at a fair market price which brought a far greater profit than could be had from an indulto. Furthermore, confiscation was more painful for the slave owners, whose entire investment was lost. It was hoped that the threat of confiscation coupled with a vigorous exercise of the right of seizure would prove an effective deterrent to the contraband trade.

But, in practice, confiscation was a failure. The factors lacked the money and the manpower to launch and maintain a sustained campaign to seize illicit slaves. The populace of the various colonies was adamantly opposed to seizures and all too often responded with violence. Then, too, the agents did not receive the active support of the royal officials, who preferred to close their eyes to infractions of the asiento contract. The company never fully appreciated the difficulties that beset its employees in their efforts to carry out this part of the contract.

The undisputed failure and inadequacy of the confiscation process to solve the problem of contraband led the factors to initiate frequent indultos in the early years of the trade. The company, however, saw the indulto at best as an easy but unsatisfactory response to the problem. Although it may be conceded that this assessment of the indulto was realistic, the factors really had no alternative, given the difficulties attendant upon the exercise of the right to seizure. To complicate matters, the company did not trust its employees and not only questioned their motives for opening indultos but doubted their ability to administer an indulto effectively. As late as 1733 two agents who opened a general indulto at Puerto del Príncipe (apparently without permission) were informed that their conduct "carrys with it the probability of a contrivance for private ends and must prove greatly to the prejudice of the Company."[29]

Scattered data provide a glimpse of the number of slaves that were indulted at some of the markets between 1716 and 1719. Table 8 gives a

TABLE 8. Number of Slaves Indulted at Selected Markets, 1716–19

Market	Number of Slaves Indulted
Cartagena	73
Trinidad	31
Santa Marta	71
Santo Domingo	10
Maracaibo	25
St. Agustín [Florida]	6
Santiago de Cuba	1
Porto Bello and Panama	246
Puerto Rico	32
Havana	124
Caracas	91
Total	710

SOURCE: AGI, Contaduría 266, ramo 3; 267, ramos 1–6; Indiferente, 2847.

breakdown of the available data and shows that Porto Bello, Panama, Havana, Caracas, and Cartagena led the other markets; unfortunately, no data exist for Buenos Aires.

It is more difficult to determine the number of slaves indulted during the 1720s and 1730s. We know that 389 slaves were indulted at Porto Bello and Panama in 1723 and 145 at Santiago de Cuba in 1733, but no other hard statistics are available. The company's financial records indicate that it received £32,249 (143,329 pesos) in net proceeds from slaves indulted between 1731 and 1736. If we assume an average profit of 50 pesos on each pieza, then 2,867 piezas had been "manifested." The number of actual slaves, as opposed to piezas, would have been a good deal more. If the average slave comprised three-quarters of a pieza, about 3,823 actual slaves were indulted during those five years.[30]

Neither seizure of contraband slaves nor indulto seems to have bothered the illicit traders very much. They sold their slaves more cheaply than the company, and their independence made them more flexible and responsive to the changing needs of the customers. In the final analysis it was the company's inflexibility and half-hearted commitment to the slave trade more than the lassitude and corruption of Spanish officials that contributed to the success of the private traders.

NOTES

1. BM, 25503, pp. 257, 289; 25504, pp. 14, 29, 31. The Royal African Company was also concerned about its own captains and crews introducing slaves clandestinely into the West Indian islands. As early as 1701 the court of assistants sternly instructed its agents to "inspect carefully all our ships that the masters or men be prevented running them ashore, and afterwards pretend they dye in the voyage." Four years later it required the captains to swear "upon the Holy Evangelists of Almighty God" that "they have not changed, landed, sold, disposed of or put out of the said ship any negro or negroes but what dyed in the voyage." But old habits persist; it may be doubted whether all captains lived up to their promises. See PRO, T70/51, p. 84; T70/58, p. 127.

2. BM, 25503, pp. 257, 289; 25504, pp. 14, 29.

3. BM, 25555, p. 23; 25564, pp. 12–24.

4. BM, 25555, p. 20; 25550, p. 105; 25563, pp. 152–53.

5. BM, 25550, p. 105; 25564, p. 85; AGI, Indiferente, 2847; Contaduría 267, ramos 1–6.

6. BM, 25564, p. 88; 25565, pp. 67–75.

7. BM, 25553, p. 85; AGI, Indiferente, 2811.

8. AGI, Indiferente, 2814, 2816.

9. BM, 25564, p. 116.

10. BM, 25563, pp. 44, 4; 25564, p. 3.

11. BM, 25555, p. 90; 25552, p. 31.

12. BM, 25554, p. 52.

13. BM, 25565, p. 65.

14. BM, 25555, p. 90.

15. BM, 25566, pp. 126–27; 32694, p. 65.

16. BM, 25564, pp. 12–24, 43–46. In 1728 the company investigated charges of corruption leveled against agents Swartz and Johnson at Panama and Porto Bello but found the men innocent; see BM, 25552, p. 29.

17. Shelburne MSS, vol. 44, 365–69; AGI, Indiferente, 2813.

18. BM, 25563, pp. 7–8; 25564, pp. 12–24.

19. BM, 25563, pp. 125–27.

20. BM, 25552, p. 8.

21. BM, 25563, pp. 125–27; 25509, p. 167.

22. BM, 25552, p. 9; 32787, p. 288.

23. These statistics are probably incomplete and should be used with caution. AGI, Contaduría 266, ramos 8, 9; 267, ramos 1–6; AGI, Indiferente, 2800–2817, 2847.

24. Agents Dennis and Cocke described how this procedure worked in Santiago de Cuba in 1733. They opened the indulto there for twelve days "at the usual price of 50 pesos per pieza, but as your Honours are obliged to pay the dutys here for all negroes you indult which is 33⅓ pesos per pieza, which with the other charges attending would yield but small profit to your Honours, we have agreed that on closing the indulto, the sum total that it produces shall be divided by 110 and the quotient to be allowed to be the number of piezas, for each of which your Honours shall pay the duty of 33⅓ pesos; that is instead of paying the above duty out of 50 pesos, you pay only so much out of 110." The sum on which the duty of 33⅓ pesos was payable was later reduced to 100 pesos. See BM, 25563, p. 40; 25564, p. 68; 25554, p. 53.

25. Of this amount the crown received 33⅓ pesos, the company 40 pesos, and the agent received the rest to cover his commission and costs. See BM, 25550, p. 99; 25563, pp. 116–22.

26. If an indulto yielded unsatisfactory results, the company had the right to ask for its reopening, although the royal officials did not always grant such requests. The agents at Cartagena complained in 1717 that their request to reopen an indulto with a lower fine per pieza had been denied. See BM, 25564, pp. 12–24; 25563, p. 162; 25554, p. 52.

27. BM, 25564, pp. 12–24; 25563, p. 162; 25554, p. 52.

28. BM, 25564, pp. 12–24.

29. BM, 25554, p. 52.

30. We are assuming that 33⅓ pesos in duty were paid on each pieza and that the remaining 16⅔ pesos went for the agent's commission and other indulto-related expenses. Shelburne MSS, vol. 43, 428–29.

6 The Distribution of the Slaves

There was much variation in the number of slaves the South Sea Company delivered to the markets of Spanish America. In terms of their needs, some colonies received a barely adequate number of slaves, others were neglected, but none was oversupplied. In fact, the company consistently failed to meet its contracted quota of annual deliveries. The ever aggressive interlopers needed no prodding to fill the lacunae. Unfortunately, since their activities were illicit, they left little in the way of records.

The number of slaves whom the British traders sold to the Spanish Americans before the asiento trade became effective cannot be precisely determined. It is known that both Jamaica and Barbados received substantial cargoes of slaves from Africa between 1680 and 1713, and that by 1700 a fair proportion of these slaves, particularly at Jamaica, were reexported to the Spanish colonies. The Royal African Company delivered 18,801 slaves at Jamaica between 1680 and 1688, and 25,287 at Barbados between 1680 and 1693. For the period 1698–1707 Jamaica obtained 44,376 slaves from the company and private traders; Barbados received 35,409 from the same sources from April 8, 1698, to April 29, 1708.[1]

A list of exports prepared from the customs records by Stephen Fuller, an eighteenth-century colonial official, gives some idea of the number of slaves transshipped from Jamaica. The records appear to err on the low side, since some traders were likely to evade the customs officials after 1707, when a duty was imposed on all slaves exported from Jamaica. Nevertheless, Fuller's list shows that at least 18,180 slaves were exported from Jamaica between 1702 and 1714, that is, before the asiento became effective. Most of these slaves presumably went to Spanish America. In contrast, Barbados exported most of its slaves during the period to other islands and to the North American colonies.[2] Barbados's distance from the Spanish markets may have precluded the development of a brisk trade with them. An estimate of the number of slaves that the English sold to the Spaniards between 1700 and 1714 might range between 1,500 and 3,000 annually.[3]

It is much easier to calculate the number of slaves that the South Sea Company's traders introduced into Spanish America under the asiento between 1714 and 1739. These records are for the most part preserved in the Archivo de Indias in Seville. There are a few lacunae; most of the shipping data for Santo Domingo and Puerto Rico have not yet been uncovered, and there are apparent gaps in some of the lists for the other markets, principally for the years immediately preceding the outbreak of the War of Jenkins' Ear. Barring these difficulties, it is possible to analyze the volume of the trade.

Most of the slave voyages to Spanish America originated in Jamaica (see Table 9). Slaves had been delivered to that island either by company ships that came from Africa or had been purchased from other traders. Of 390 ships for which the point of origin is available, 231 (59 percent) sailed from Jamaica. The ships which originated in Africa delivered their slaves principally at Buenos Aires and to a lesser extent at Cartagena and Porto Bello.[4] Barbadian ships for the most part sailed in the early years of the asiento or in the 1730s.

Many of the ships that went to Caracas, particularly after 1722, came from the islands of St. Christopher, Curaçao, and St. Eustatius. The latter two islands were quite close to the Venezuelan coast and the South Sea Company found it convenient to buy slaves there from the Dutch. A high proportion of the vessels that originated in the islands were small sloops, brigs, and packet boats, each carrying fewer than fifty slaves at a time; slightly larger ships carried a hundred more or less. The standard slave ships of 250 and 300 tons' burden transported in excess of 200 slaves at a time. Some ships that brought supplies for the factories also carried a few slaves, usually no more than ten and often fewer.

One complication in the records is that the Spaniards did not calculate slaves by individual heads but by piezas. To determine the number of piezas in a cargo, the slaves had to be "measured" or "regulated." As soon as the examining physician had released a cargo of slaves, two or more royal officials came aboard to initiate the "regulation" process. The contract required that all slaves be measured within fifteen days of arrival.

The height, age, and physical condition of the captive were crucial

TABLE 9. Origins of 390 Slave Vessels to Spanish
America, 1715–38

Place of Origin	Number of Vessels	Percentage
Angola	32	8.2
Gold Coast	9	2.3
Madagascar	6	1.5
Whydah	6	1.5
Jamaica	231	59.2
Barbados	33	8.5
St. Christopher	39	10.0
Curaçao	21	5.4
St. Eustatius	3	0.8
African coast in general	10	2.6
Total	390	100.0

SOURCE: AGI, Contaduría, 267, 268; Indiferente, 2800–2817.

factors to be taken into consideration by the royal officers. Before the actual measuring began, the slaves who were not suffering from a serious illness or severe disability were divided into four groups, according to age and sex. The first two groups consisted of men and women who appeared to be at least fifteen years old. Boys and girls of fourteen or less made up the other two groups. There might also be other assorted groups that comprised slaves who were obviously ill.

The slave's height was determined first. The unit of measurement was the palmo, roughly equivalent to eight and a half inches. In general, a slave who measured seven palmos (just under five feet) was declared to be a pieza de India; however, a slave might measure less than seven palmos and still be classified as a pieza if he were at least fifteen years old and healthy. Slaves with serious physical impairments such as a missing arm or eye or who were ill with, say, smallpox might be counted as three-fourths or one-half or one-third, and so on, of a pieza. Or a slave considered too old (usually over thirty) might not be evaluated as a pieza but as a fraction of one. A minor disability—a missing finger, a toe, or a tooth—did not normally require a reduction, provided he met the other criteria of health, age, and stature. An exceptional boy or girl of thirteen or fourteen who was physically well developed and in good health might be measured as a pieza, but minors usually were counted as fractions. Infants were measured with their mothers. Finally, mentally unbalanced or elderly slaves (over fifty) were not measured at all.

A slave who had been measured but who died before the expiration of fifteen days was not counted in the final tally of piezas landed. As a rule, slaves seriously ill at the time of the officials' visit were not measured, since some were expected to die. However, it was mandatory that the survivors, regardless of physical condition, be measured on the fifteenth day. When measurement was completed, the total number of piezas was credited to the company's account as part of the 4,800 piezas the asiento required it to deliver annually.

There was much room for argument in the measurement process. The Spanish crown liked the highest measurement, since it collected a duty of $33\frac{1}{3}$ pesos on each pieza. The company's interest, though it was slow to realize it, was best served by a low measurement, since the more slaves that constituted a pieza the lower the actual duty per slave. Retail sales were still to be negotiated, and a shrewd agent could persuade the customers to pay a higher price for a slave than the official measurement would have indicated.

Sometimes the factor's protests over a measurement could induce the local authorities to revise the evaluation. In 1716, for example, the agents at Panama were outraged to learn that a cargo of 347 slaves comprised 337 piezas; a second measurement reduced the piezas to 287, or 50 fewer. At times the company was dismayed at the results of the measurements. In 1716 it complained to the factors at Vera Cruz that "the regulation of 73 negro men and 1 negro woman brought by the St. George at $73\frac{2}{3}$ piezas seems to us to be extraordinary." The letter went on to advise the factors to "endeavour to obtain as much indulgence of the Royal Officers in the measurement of our negroes as you can, the usual measurement is 3 for 4, but we would not have here be understood that you should pay their favour." The following year the court of directors grumbled about 156 slaves, including many women and children, who had been measured at $142\frac{4}{7}$ piezas at Cartagena.[5]

As the company's 1716 letter to the Vera Cruz factors indicated, measurement was not considered important enough to justify the expense of bribes. The company had to provide 4,800 piezas per year anyway, and its slave supplies were so limited that it could not run much above that figure no matter how the slaves were measured. This reasoning led the court of directors to tell the agents in Buenos Aires in 1717 that low measurements were "no benefit." The company's policy, it must be said, was ill informed

TABLE 10. Measurement of 437 Slaves, Buenos Aires, 1725

Number of Slaves	Sex	Measurement	Number of Piezas
67	M	1 pieza each	67
25	M	⅘ pieza each	20
84	M	⅔ pieza each	56
92	M	½ pieza each	46
76 (8 with babies)	F	1 pieza each	76
12	F	⅘ pieza each	9⅗
35	F	⅔ pieza each	23½
24	F	½ pieza each	12
2 (sick)	M	1 pieza each	2
13	M	⅔ pieza each	8⅔
2	F	1 pieza each	2
5	F	⅔ pieza each	3⅓
Total 437			325¹⁴⁄₁₅

SOURCE: AGI, Contaduría 268, ramo 11.

and inconsistent. At the very time it was telling the Buenos Aires factors that low measurements were of no benefit, it was berating the employees at Vera Cruz for accepting high measurements and was urging them "to get as many negroes allowed for a pieza de India as possible."[6]

In the early years the company did not fully realize that the officials' measurement of a slave was virtually irrelevant to his selling price. When it finally understood that buyers made their own evaluation and that price also depended on the factor's salesmanship, the court of directors decided that the company's interest was better served by low measurements whether or not it supplied 4,800 piezas annually. Still, it considered bribes in return for low measurements a waste of money. In 1729 we find the agents at Panama and Porto Bello being instructed "to get as many negroes allowed for a pieza as you can but not to give any fees to obtain it."[7]

It may be instructive to examine in some detail the measurement of two cargoes of slaves (see Table 10). The *Syrria* reached Buenos Aires in 1725 with a cargo of 440 slaves, 160 of whom were women and 280 men. Three of the seven women were suffering from "great weakness"; of the men who were ill, one had but one leg. There were 437 slaves who were believed well enough to be measured, and these amounted to 324^{14}/$_{15}$ piezas de Indias. The second example of measurement is the *Asiento*'s cargo of 295 slaves to Buenos Aires in 1725 (see Table 11). Fifteen died soon after arriving, two were too ill to be measured, and the remaining 278 (168 males and 110 females) amounted to 208^{5}/$_{6}$ piezas. As these two examples demonstrate, the number of piezas in a given cargo could be considerably less than the total number of individual slaves. Both tables bear out the company's assumption that the normal ratio of piezas to slaves was three to four.

The number of individual slaves that arrived, in contradistinction to the number of piezas they constituted, provides a more easily understood picture of the patterns of distribution. Existing records make possible a port-by-port accounting of slave arrivals between 1714 and 1739.[8] Table 12 shows that the factories at Porto Bello and Panama received 19,662 slaves between 1715 and 1738. These were the two most active centers of the trade; a substantial proportion of these slaves went to Lima and to various areas on the Pacific coast of South America. The Buenos Aires factory, as shown in Table 13, received the second largest number of slaves:

TABLE 11. Measurement of 278 Slaves, Buenos Aires, 1725

Number of Slaves	Sex	Measurement	Number of Piezas
50	M	1 pieza each	50
52	M	¾ pieza each	39
42	M	½ pieza each	21
25	F	1 pieza each	25
41	F	⅔ pieza each	27⅓
21	F	½ pieza each	10½
9 (sick)	M	1 pieza each	9
15 (sick)	M	½ pieza each	7½
16 (sick)	F	1 pieza each	16
7 (sick)	F	½ pieza each	3½
Total 278			208⅚

SOURCE: AGI, Contaduría 268, ramo 13.

TABLE 12. Slaves to Panama and Porto Bello, 1715–38

Year	Number of Ships	Number of Slaves
1715	1	150
1716	4	911
1717	5	1,093
1718	8	1,584
1722	5	890
1722		5*
1723	6	1,408
1724	7	1,676
1725	6	1,646
1726	5	588
1727	1	299
1729	2	214
1730	5	1,328
1731	9	2,075
1732	5	1,518
1733	5	1,213
1734	2	271
1735	5	1,047
1736	4	897
1737	2	699
1738	1	150
Total	88	19,662

SOURCE: AGI, Contaduría 267, ramos 2, 8; 268, ramo 3; Indiferente, 2810, 2812, 2813, 2815, 2816.

*These slaves arrived on four cargo vessels.

16,222 between 1715 and 1738. As noted, these slaves were destined both for the port city itself and the interior provinces of contemporary Argentina and for Bolivia, Chile, and parts of Peru.

The factory at Cartagena received the third largest number (see Table 14). The company delivered 10,549 slaves there between 1714 and 1736. Most of them were destined for the interior region of the viceroyalty of New Granada, where they were used in households, haciendas, and the mines.

Havana ranked fourth; the records (see Table 15) indicate that at least 6,387 slaves were landed there by the company between 1715 and 1738.

TABLE 13. Slaves to Buenos Aires, 1715–38

Year	Number of Ships	Number of Slaves
1715	2	616
1716	3	758
1717	3	633
1718	4	1,158
1719	1	208
1722	1	370
1723	3	1,388
1724	4	1,340
1725	4	1,520
1726	3	1,102
1727	2	521
1728	1	135
1730	5	1,921
1731	4	1,432
1732	2	1,085
1734	1	448
1736	2	658
1737	1	357
1738	2	572
Total	48	16,222

SOURCE: AGI, Contaduría 268, ramo 7; Indiferente, 2800.

Statistics for the factory at Santiago de Cuba are incomplete, but it is known that 456 slaves were disembarked there between 1716 and 1718, and 520 between 1731 and 1733. If these figures are typical of the period, Santiago handled about one-fourth to one-third as much business as its larger counterpart at Havana.[9]

The remaining two factories—at Vera Cruz and Caracas—received the smallest number of slaves. The records show that Caracas admitted 5,240 slaves from 82 vessels in the company's service between 1715 and 1739 (see Table 16). Vera Cruz had considerably less business, receiving only 3,011 slaves between 1716 and 1739 (see Table 17).

Additional records give the number of slaves sold at some of the markets where no factories existed. Table 18 shows that Maracaibo received 563 slaves between 1717 and 1734, while Campeche received 805 between 1725 and 1739 (see Table 19). Some of Campeche's slaves went to

Guatemala and other parts of Mexico. Santa Marta, a small market, received only 222 slaves from the company's ships between 1725 and 1735. It is impossible to provide a statistical picture of the company's trade with Guatemala, Puerto Rico, and Santo Domingo, since only a few of the relevant records are extant. We only know that Guatemala received 162 slaves between 1731 and 1733, while Santo Domingo received 103 and Puerto Rico 115 during the same period. These were not major trade centers, so a reasonable estimate for the three might be in the neighborhood of an additional 1,260 slaves between 1717 and 1730.[10]

Synthesizing the statistical information, we can say that the company delivered a known total of 64,017 slaves at Panama and Porto Bello, Buenos Aires, Cartagena, Caracas, Vera Cruz, Guatemala, Puerto Rico, Santo Domingo, Havana, Santiago de Cuba, Maracaibo, Santa Marta, and Campeche. Another 1,260 may have been delivered at Santo Domin-

TABLE 14. Slaves to Cartagena, 1714–36

Year	Number of Ships	Number of Slaves
1714	1	174
1715	1	283
1716	3	313
1717	5	349
1718	3	291
1722	4	480
1723	3	789
1724	5	789
1725	5	1,298
1726	3	420
1727	3	320
1730	4	731
1731	5	1,077
1732	5	718
1733	4	700
1734	5	840
1735	4	401
1736	5	576
Total	68	10,549

SOURCE: AGI, Contaduría 267, ramo 1; 268, ramo 2; Indiferente, 2809, 2813.

TABLE 15. Slaves to Havana, 1715–38

Year	Number of Ships	Number of Slaves
1715	3	238
1716	6	365
1717	6	467
1718	5	348
1722	1	170
1723	4	204
1724	5	289
1725	8	637
1726	6	576
1727	2	150
1729	1	69
1730	5	630
1731	10	1,105
1732	8	656
1733	2	76
1734	3	32
1736	4	230
1737	4	75
1738	1	70
Total	84	6,387

SOURCE: AGI, Contaduría 268, ramo 4; Indiferente, 2786, 2809, 2812, 2815, 2816.

go, Guatemala, and Puerto Rico. And it may be guessed that Santiago de Cuba received about 783 slaves from 1722 to 1730 and from 1734 to 1739, or about one-fourth of the number Havana received during these years. The other areas on the Windward Coast like Cumaná and Trinidad, being small and poor, may have received no more than 800 slaves throughout the period. Thus it is possible to make a cautious estimate of 66,860 slaves landed by the South Sea Company between 1714 and 1739 (see Table 20).

This estimate, of course, does not include the prize slaves or those indulted or confiscated. The paucity of records makes difficult even a tentative estimate of this branch of the trade. Based on the scattered data available on the prize slaves (mentioned earlier), it may be conjectured that about 1,000 slaves were seized by the Spanish and handed over to the company during the period. Statistics relative to the size of the indultos are generally lacking for the 1720s and 1730s. As Table 8 showed, 710 slaves were indulted at various markets between 1716 and 1719. We have also suggested that about 3,823 slaves were indulted between 1731 and 1736. Since the practice of opening indultos never ceased throughout the period, one can speculate that, overall, about 6,500 slaves were added to the company's account by this means. The number of illicit slaves confiscated by the company's factors is the most difficult of all to estimate. Occasionally slaves were seized, but, as noted, their owners sometimes wrested them away from the agents. It is probably not too far wrong to estimate that no

TABLE 16. Slaves to Caracas, 1715–39

Year	Number of Ships	Number of Slaves
1715	3	249
1716	1	30
1717	3	44
1718	6	165
1722	4	131
1723	7	228
1724	7	170
1725	4	51
1726	5	164
1727	3	80
1728	1	30
1729	5	215
1730	5	388
1731	4	528
1732	8	569
1733	6	556
1734	1	92
1735	2	300
1736	2	280
1737	2	375
1738	2	372
1739	1	223
Total	82	5,240

SOURCE: AGI, Contaduría 268, ramo 8; Indiferente, 2801, 2810, 2811, 2815, 2817; Shelburne MSS, vol. 43, 127.

TABLE 17. Slaves to Vera Cruz, 1716–39

Year	Number of Ships	Number of Slaves
1716	2	116
1717	2	280
1718	1	96
1719	1	30
1722	1	72
1723	3	272
1724	2	360
1725	2	150
1726	3	88
1727	3	85
1729	2	109
1730	2	133
1731	1	100
1732	3	244
1733	3	95
1734	1	100
1735	1	101
1736	2	100
1737	2	100
1738	4	280
1739	1	100
Total	42	3,011

SOURCE: AGI, Contaduría 268, ramo 1; Indiferente, 2786, 2807, 2809–11, 2815, 2817, 2818.

more than 400 slaves were seized by the factors throughout the period of the asiento trade. The estimated number of slaves who were prize, indulted, or confiscated thus stands at 7,900. The overall total of slaves introduced under the company's aegis can now be estimated at 74,760.

The extant records make it possible to calculate the male-female ratio of the company's slave cargoes between 1715 and 1738. In a sample of 17,080 slaves who arrived in Spanish America during that period, 11,321 (66.28 percent) were males. This sex ratio reflects the traders' objective of delivering at least two males for every female.[11] Interestingly, this ratio also conforms roughly to that found for other branches of the slave trade. A study of the trade conducted by the Netherlands West India Company be-

TABLE 18. Slaves to Maracaibo, 1717–34

Year	Number of Ships	Number of Slaves
1717	1	80
1718	2	67
1724	1	53
1726	1	20
1727	1	50
1729	1	27
1730	3	64
1731	1	24
1732	2	106
1733	2	55
1734	1	17
Total	16	563

SOURCE: AGI, Contaduría 268, ramo 5; Indiferente, 2811.

TABLE 19. Slaves to Campeche, 1725–39

Year	Number of Ships	Number of Slaves
1725	2	41
1726	1	27
1730	3	60
1731	4	75
1732	4	73
1733	1	12
1734	2	150
1735	2	150
1737	1	17
1738	1	100
1739	1	100
Total	22	805

SOURCE: AGI, Indiferente, 2786; Shelburne MSS, vol. 43, 247.

TABLE 20. Estimates of Slaves Delivered to Spanish America by the South Sea
Company, 1714–39

Period	Port or Country of Entry	Number of Slaves (Known Arrivals)	
1715–38	Panama and Porto Bello	19,662	
1715–38	Buenos Aires	16,222	
1714–36	Cartagena	10,549	
1715–38	Havana	6,387	
1716–18, 1731–33	Santiago de Cuba	976	
1715–39	Caracas	5,240	
1716–39	Vera Cruz	3,011	
1713–34	Maracaibo	563	
1725–39	Campeche	805	
1725–35	Santa Marta	222	
1731–33	Guatemala	162	
1731–33	Puerto Rico	115	
1731–33	Santo Domingo	103	
Subtotal		64,017	
		(Estimated Arrivals)	
1716–30	Guatemala, Santo Domingo, Puerto Rico	1,260	
1722–30, 1734–39	Santiago de Cuba	783	
1716–39	Trinidad, Cumaná, Margarita, etc.	800	
Subtotal		2,843	
		(Confiscated, Prize, and Indulted Slaves)	
1715–39	All of Spanish America	1,000	(Prize)
		6,500	(Indulted)
		400	(Confiscated)
Subtotal		7,900	
Total		74,760	

SOURCE: Calculations based on Tables 13, 14–24.

tween 1681 and 1751 found that 29 percent of the slaves carried were female and 71 percent male. For the English slave trade to Jamaica between
1791 and 1798, the ratio was 38 percent female to 62 percent male.[12]

The South Sea Company never at any time met its annual contractual
obligation of 4,800 piezas. During the twenty-two years of actual trad-

ing between 1714 and 1739, the company should have delivered about 105,600 piezas, or the rough equivalent of 140,800 slaves.[13] My analysis suggests that the average annual introduction was 3,398 slaves. If the four war years are included, the figure falls to 2,875. No attempt is made to compute the size of the illicit trade, but it may have amounted to about one-third to one-half of the company's annual trade.

These data may be usefully compared with those advanced in Curtin's *The Atlantic Slave Trade*. Using information derived from secondary authorities, Curtin suggested that Spanish America received an annual average of 3,880 slaves during the years 1641–1773.[14] These figures are not significantly different from those that I have attributed to the company during the years of active trading. On the other hand, Curtin's statistics are not confined to deliveries made by the South Sea Company but include all the slaves supplied to the Spaniards, legally and illegally. In view of the known annual deliveries that the company made and the extent of the contraband trade, it seems safe to conclude that Curtin's calculations are too low for the asiento years.

The South Sea Company, it must be conceded, exercised much prudence in selecting the slaves it sent to Spanish America. Yet one may doubt whether the court of directors ever made a bona fide effort to supply the colonists with all the slaves they needed. After the South Sea Bubble burst, the company became less interested in commerce, and whatever energies it could muster seem to have been expended chiefly on the annual ships and the contraband trade. Seen in this light, the company acted in bad faith in its dealings with the Spaniards; whether the Spaniards deserved better is a matter of opinion.

NOTES

1. PRO, T70/175, pp. 15, 10–11, 135.

2. For Jamaica's exports, see CO, vol. 137, no. 38, 5. Jamaica's interisland export trade does not appear to have been very extensive at this time. For a discussion of Barbadian export patterns, see Rudnyanszky, "The Caribbean Slave Trade," pp. 207–11.

3. In 1708 the private traders claimed that in the three previous years they had sold between 6,000 and 7,000 slaves annually to the Spaniards. This figure may have been exaggerated for the purpose of convincing the British Parliament to introduce completely free trade. See PRO, T70/175, p. 27.

4. Unfortunately, information on the precise port of origin in Africa is not available for some of these ships; hence they are listed in Table 9 as coming from the "African coast."

5. BM, 25563, pp. 18, 7–8, 44, 86.

6. BM, 25563, pp. 102, 57.

7. BM, 25566, p. 74. In 1736 the court of directors reminded its agents at Vera Cruz to "sell slaves by the head and not according to piezas." See AGI, Indiferente, 2814.

8. The figures given here represent the tally made when the slaves were measured. They do not include the number that died prior to that time. Hence there may be minor differences between these figures and those given in the earlier discussions on mortality rates.

9. AGI, Contaduría 266, ramo 10; 267, ramos 4, 8; Indiferente, 2847.

10. The average number of slaves these three areas received between 1731 and 1733 was 126. Assuming that this average was constant throughout the effective period of the license trade (1717–33), those areas would have received about 1,638 slaves during the thirteen trading years. The four war years are excluded from my calculations.

11. AGI, Indiferente, 2817; Contaduría 267, ramos 1–8; de Studer, *La trata de negros*, p. 234.

12. Johannes Postma, "The Dutch Participation in the African Slave Trade, 1675–1795" (Ph.D. thesis, Michigan State University, 1970), pp. 177–78; Klein, *Middle Passage*, p. 149.

13. Specifically, these years include 1714–18, 1722–27, 1729–39. The company delivered 208 slaves at Buenos Aires in 1719 and 30 at Caracas in 1728— both war years. I have not included these two years and the 238 slaves in my calculation of the annual average, however, since trade was suspended for the greater portion of these years.

14. Curtin, *Atlantic Slave Trade*, pp. 23–25.

7 Health, Age, and Prices

Spanish Americans, like other New World buyers, were in the market for the healthiest and strongest slave, one who would live long enough to repay the investment and yield a profit. Slave traders, in their turn, were only too aware that the age, state of health, and physical appearance of their slaves were intimately related to the price obtainable for each one. As businessmen they also recognized that their profits depended on whether their slaves could survive the hazards of new diseases in the Americas, new diet, and the lingering physical disability and psychological trauma of the Atlantic passage.[1]

Since epidemics so often followed the arrival of slave cargoes, the authorities in the New World took steps to minimize the danger. In Jamaica, for example, a cargo was normally quarantined for eight days, presumably to isolate the sick from the local population and the slaves already in the pens. The asiento contract forbade the English traders to disembark slaves on Spanish American soil before a medical examination had been made. Medical personnel would board a newly arrived ship to check both slaves and crew for communicable diseases. At their discretion, the captain could be refused permission to land until the risk of infection disappeared. In most cases the quarantine period was two weeks or less; in rare instances the ship and its cargo would be sent to an isolated island until the disease had run its course. The medical inspection of the *Elizabeth*, which reached Caracas on March 11, 1737, found eleven cases of smallpox. The English factor reported that one of the slaves had "the smallpox green upon him, which the doctors insisted to have been sufficient to infect the rest." The ship was quarantined on one of the tiny cluster of islands, known collectively as the Aves or Bird Islands, off the Venezuelan coast.[2]

The physicians' judgment was vindicated; in a little over a month 130 slaves on the *Elizabeth* contracted smallpox, but only five (two men, one woman, and two girls) died. The ship was held at Aves for forty days after the last victim recovered, and during the quarantine other diseases took a steady toll. Some thirty-two slaves suffered from dysentery and seven of them died. Two men died from "malignant fevers" (probably malaria), and another man succumbed to an "imposthume in the lungs" (probably pneumonia). One girl died of apoplexy. Three persons with dropsy and four others with venereal disease apparently recovered. In all, 182 slaves came down with one malady or another during their stay on Aves, and of these seventeen died. Agent Butcher's one item of good news during this wretched period was that "one of the finest women had been delivered of a mulatto boy and were both well."[3]

The Spanish residents of port cities were often terror-stricken by rumors that a slave cargo was infected with a contagious disease. One trader wrote from Caracas in 1737: "The fears of the people in regard to smallpox is so great that on the first appearance of it, every family that is able leaves the city." In his opinion the smallpox brought by the slave ships, particularly from Barbados, "proves most fatall to them [the Spaniards] and their families." There is reason to believe that the Spaniards may not have acquired any immunity, and even those who survived were permanently scarred. Agent John Merewether noted that "American Spaniards . . . have the smallpox in the utmost terror and the reason why it proves so fatal to them is that few of them are clear of the great pox, or its attendants."[4]

Since an outbreak of smallpox could ruin sales, the traders did everything they could to minimize the risk. The South Sea Company's agents at Jamaica tried, often without success, to prevent shipboard infection. Merewether's handling of the *Santa Clara* in 1738 is a case in point. He reported that he was "at present under a good deal of care about the negroes, the smallpox increase greatly . . . the Santa Clara was smoakt with brimston and tar before the negroes were put on board, and the vessel ordered to the keys to prevent the smallpox breaking out." The captain was directed to sail to Havana if there was no outbreak within seven days, but a few days later twenty-six slaves were infected "and more falling down," as Merewether put it.[5]

Although smallpox was common in every part of the trade, from the African settlements to the Spanish Americas, there was no reliable method of preventing or treating it. According to the agents in the 1730s, slaves who were even temporarily landed at Barbados were likely to contract smallpox. The unhealthy climate was often blamed, but Thomas Butcher at Caracas in 1737 was convinced that the "victualling" of the slaves at Barbados was "very indifferent and not fitt to keep them in good condition and health, it being chiefly Indian corn not ground, boyld with a little bit of ordinary Irish beeffe . . . neither had they a proper conveniency of yard room for a number of negroes to keep them in health." Until inoculation became more common in the late eighteenth century, Butcher's prescription was perhaps as good as any.[6]

Although smallpox was the most feared, many other ailments and disabilities reduced the salability of black cargoes. When the *Charles* arrived in Cartagena from Jamaica in 1714 with 174 slaves, the examining physician found fifty-six of them sick or defective in some way. Some had several teeth or a finger or two missing; others had impaired vision, ulcers

TABLE 21. Diseases and Disabilities of 56 Slaves on the *Charles*, Cartagena, 1714

Diseases and Disabilities	Number of Slaves Affected		Number of Cases
	Male	Female	
Genitourinary diseases			
Venereal	2	1	3
Prolapse of the uterus		2	2
Eye diseases and disabilities			
Impaired vision	8		8
Blind in one eye	1		1
Musculoskeletal disabilities			
Hernia	3	1	4
Teeth missing	8		8
Fingers missing	7	1	8
Skin diseases			
Ulcers and sores	6	1	7
Rashes	1	2	3
Ringworm		3	3
Miscellaneous			
Thin (*flaco*)	2	3	5
Scurvy	1		1
Sleeping sickness		1	1
Guinea worm		2	2
Unidentified		2	2

SOURCE: AGI, Indiferente, 2800.

TABLE 22. Health and Mortality of Slaves Arriving at Buenos Aires, 1715–38

Year	Ship	Place of Origin	Number Arriving	Number of Sick	Percentage of Sick	Number Dead within 15 Days	Percentage of Deaths
1715	Europe	Angola	372	Unknown	Unknown	12	3.2
1716	Indian Queen	Angola	289	77	26.6	7	2.4
1716	Prince of Wales	Angola	307	48	15.6	7	2.3
1716	Windsor	Angola	162	73	45.1	31	19.1
1717	Kingston	Angola	188	50	26.6	14	7.5
1717	Sarah Gally	Madagascar	347	18	5.2	5	1.4
1717	George	Angola	243	Unknown	Unknown	145	59.7
1718	St. Quintin	Angola	294	14	4.8	1	0.3
1718	Europe	Whydah	310	Unknown	Unknown	2	0.7
1718	Thomas and Deborah	Whydah	285	32	11.2	15	5.3
1718	Crown	Angola	284	1	0.4	1	0.4
1719	Arabella	Madagascar	208	33	15.9	8	3.9
1722	Asiento	Gold Coast	370	19	5.1	2	0.5
1723	King William	Angola	555	42	7.6	17	3.1
1723	St. Quintin	Angola [?]	295	30	10.2	8	2.7
1724	Carteret	Angola	295	18	6.1	—	—
1724	Sea Horse	Angola	304	17	5.6	—	—
1724	Essex	Angola	375	33	8.8	8	2.1
1724	Levantine	Angola	366	11	3.0	1	0.3
1725	Syrria	Angola	440	22	5.0	6	1.4
1725	Asiento	Angola	295	47	15.9	21	7.1
1725	Wootle	Angola	425	22	5.2	22	5.2
1725	Erith	Angola	360	25	6.9	8	2.2

Year	Ship	Place of Origin	Number Arriving	Number of Sick	Percentage of Sick	Number Dead within 15 Days	Percentage of Deaths
1726	Beautiful	Angola	444	6	1.4	1	0.2
1726	Duke of Cambridge	Angola	458	35	7.6	16	3.5
1726	Essex	Angola	200	13	6.5	6	3.0
1727	King William	Angola	239	7	2.9	5	2.1
1727	St. Michael	Madagascar	282	26	9.2	1	0.4
1728	Sea Horse	Madagascar	135	65	48.2	30	22.2
1730	Mermaid	Angola	579	10	1.7	3	0.5
1730	Rudge	Madagascar	244	40	16.4	Unknown	Unknown
1730	St. Michael	Madagascar	267	43	16.1	12	4.5
1731	Beautiful	Angola	431	5	1.2	8	1.9
1731	Laurence	Angola	394	17	4.3	10	2.5
1731	City of London	Whydah	381	33	8.7	17	4.5
1731	Eaton	Angola	226	22	9.7	19	8.4
1732	Mermaid	Angola	551	6	1.1	6	1.1
1732	Princess Emelia	Angola	542	8	1.5	8	1.5
1734	Rudge	Angola	448	12	2.7	3	0.7
1736	Hiscox	Angola	254	Unknown	Unknown	11	4.3
1736	Anne	Angola	404	Unknown	Unknown	7	1.7
1737	Genoa	Angola [?]	357	7	2.0	10	2.8
1738	Asiento	Angola	283	7	2.5	3	1.1
1738	Asia	Angola	289	18	6.2	5	1.7

SOURCE: AGI, Indiferente, 2809; de Studer, *La trata de negros*, p. 235; BM, 25494–584.

TABLE 23. Health of Slaves Arriving at Porto Bello, 1716–25

Year	Ship	Place of Origin	Number Arriving	Number of Sick	Percentage of Sick
1716	*Dunwich Merchant*	Whydah and Jamaica	347	25	7.2
1716	*Pearl*	Gold Coast	147	17	0.1
1716	*King Solomon*	Gold and Windward coasts	287	20	7.0
1717	*Dragon*	Jamaica	210	16	7.6
1717	*St. James*	Jamaica	250	8	3.2
1717	*John*	Jamaica	188	5	2.7
1717	*Greenbay*	Jamaica	186	11	6.0
1717	*Indian Queen*	Africa* and Jamaica	259	9	3.5
1718	*Neptune*	Jamaica	200	20	10.0
1718	*John*	Gold Coast and Jamaica	283	41	14.5
1718	*Aguila*	Jamaica	135	14	10.4
1718	*Crown*	Africa* and Jamaica	218	5	2.3
1718	*Friendship*	Barbados	110	4	3.6
1718	*John*	Africa* and Barbados	183	43	23.5
1718	*George Augustus*	Whydah and Jamaica	266	13	4.9
1722	*Asiento*	Jamaica	173	13	7.5
1722	*Fame*	Jamaica	189	12	6.4
1722	*Prince of Asturias*	Jamaica	231	12	5.2
1722	*St. George*	Jamaica	199	7	3.5
1722	*Charles*	Jamaica	279	7	2.5
1723	*Prince of Asturias*	Jamaica	162	6	3.7
1724	*Prince of Asturias*	Jamaica	126	6	4.8
1724	*Prince of Asturias*	Jamaica	280	1	0.4
1724	*Prince of Asturias*	Jamaica	280	2	0.8
1724	*Queen of Spain*	Jamaica	220	23	10.5
1725	*St. George*	Jamaica	365	2	0.6
1725	*Charles*	Jamaica	296	2	0.7
	Total		6,069	344	5.7

SOURCE: AGI, Indiferente, 2810.

* "Africa" is used here in a general sense because the place of origin is not recorded.

and sores, hernias, prolapse of the uterus, scurvy, venereal disease, Guinea worms, and ringworm. Table 21 presents the details.[7]

The health problems of slave cargoes probably caused more trouble at Buenos Aires than elsewhere, since all its cargoes came directly from Africa. No ship arrived without at least some sick slaves, and there was hardly a cargo in which two or more slaves did not die within fifteen days of arrival. Table 22 gives data on some of these arrivals for the years 1715–38.[8]

The statistics for Porto Bello during the period 1716–25 provide basis for comparison with Buenos Aires regarding the health of the arriving slaves (Table 23). It is noteworthy that the ships from Africa which had stopped in Jamaica or Barbados to "refresh" their slaves and to purchase healthier ones to replace the seriously ill were carrying 136 sick slaves out of 1,556 (8.7 percent) when they docked at Porto Bello. The table also shows that two ships that came directly from Africa to Porto Bello arrived with thirty-seven sick in a cargo of 434 (8.5 percent). Taken together, these eight ships brought 1,990 slaves, of whom 173 (8.7 percent) were ill.

By contrast, the vessels that had originated in Jamaica or Barbados had a sickness rate of only 4.2 percent (171 of 4,079). It is true that agents in the islands generally held back ill or maimed slaves from these deliveries, but the figures also suggest that slaves who remained in Jamaica or Barbados long enough to recuperate from the Atlantic passage were less likely to fall ill on the shorter voyage to Spanish America. Overall, 344 (5.7 percent) of the 6,069 slaves in the sample were ill when their ships anchored at Porto Bello. For Buenos Aires the proportion of slaves arriving sick was higher. In a sample of 13,194 slaves who came from Africa between 1715 and 1738, 1,012 (7.7 percent) disembarked ill (Table 22).

It is certain that a significant number of slaves died in port before being sold. Hence it was to the trader's advantage to dispose of his captives quickly. The life expectancy of a group of slaves depended on certain factors: general health, care, and diet after capture and the disease environment encountered. Buenos Aires, Porto Bello, and Panama were considered the most unhealthy regions of Spanish America; consequently the mortality rate was highest in these places.

Table 22 gives the death rate for a sample of ships' cargoes for the first fifteen days after arrival at Buenos Aires. Table 24 details the mortality rate of the slaves prior to sale for the thirteen ships that arrived between 1715 and 1719.[9] It is obvious that many more died after the first fifteen

TABLE 24. Mortality of Slaves Arriving at Buenos Aires, 1715–19

Year	Ship	Number in Cargo*	Number before Sale	Percentage before Sale
1715	Wiltshire	247	6	2.4
1715	Europe	373	37	9.9
1716	Indian Queen	290	11	3.8
1716	Prince of Wales	305	30	9.8
1716	Windsor	162	42	25.9
1717	Hope [Kingston]	188	40	21.3
1717	Sarah Gally	347	17	4.9
1717	George	243	148	60.9
1718	St. Quintin	294	11	3.7
1718	Europe	312	35	11.2
1718	Thomas and Deborah	281	61	21.7
1718	Crown	285	47	16.5
1719	Arabella	212	15	7.1
Total		3,539	500	14.1

SOURCES: AGI, Contaduría 267, ramo 6; Indiferente, 2809.

*In some instances Tables 22 and 24 show different figures for the arriving cargoes of slaves. These discrepancies are not very significant statistically and probably reflect clerical errors.

days. The *Prince of Wales*'s 1716 cargo, for example, lost seven in the first fifteen days and twenty-three more before sale; in the next year the *Sarah* lost five in the first fifteen days and twelve more subsequently. In summation, the 7.5 percent death rate in the first fifteen days climbed to 14.1 percent before the slaves could be sold in this early period. The mortality became even greater in the later period. The company's records show that of 3,800 slaves on hand between October, 1730, and October, 1736, 1,124 died, a disastrous 29.6 percent. In contrast to Buenos Aires, only eighty-two (5.8 percent) of the slaves that arrived in Cartagena between 1714 and 1718 died before they were sold.[10]

The mortality rate before sale would have been even higher had not the majority of the slaves been young. Slave masters in Spanish America, at least during the asiento years, generally preferred slaves between the ages of ten and twenty-five. Few were willing to invest in children under ten who might die before doing any productive work. Nor was there much demand for slaves over twenty-five, and a slave in his thirties or forties was

TABLE 25. Estimated Ages of 53 Slaves on the
Elizabeth, 1737

Age	Male	Female	Total
30–35	9	5	14
36–40	13	3	16
41–45	10	0	10
46–50	11	1	12
51 and over	1	0	1

SOURCE: Shelburne MSS, vol. 44, 631–32.

practically unsalable. Life expectancy in the period, especially for slaves, was far too short to justify investing in labor past its youth.

Agents were often driven to their wits' end to fill a cargo with prime young slaves, and they frequently had to gamble with undesirable cargoes. In 1737, for example, the *Elizabeth* reached Caracas with some slaves who, according to agent Peter Burrell, were "so very old and ordinary that none cared to buy them." He described some of the men as having "gray hairs on their heads and beards." When the agents in Venezuela denounced the elderly cargo as "not saleable," the Barbados factors who had assembled the cargo vehemently asserted that the slaves were really young, and that smallpox, coupled with "an ill state of health," had produced "alterations" in "their countenances," thereby making them look older than they were. Table 25 shows the estimated ages of fifty-three of the *Elizabeth*'s slaves.[11]

A cargo containing so many old slaves was unusual. The majority of slave cargoes appears to have had an average age of twenty or less.[12] The average age of the slaves on the *Margarita*, which arrived in Vera Cruz in 1734, for example, was only 13.4 years. Table 26 not only shows the ages and sexual composition of the cargo but provides a chilling picture of the impact of the trade on the very young. An analysis of the data on 970 slaves (see Table 27) who arrived in Spanish America between 1715 and 1735 yields an average age of 17.5 years.[13] (The calculation does not include children under five, most of whom were described as babies. Their number cannot have been large enough to lower the average significantly.) The average age of the females was eighteen and that of the males was seventeen, and it should also be noted that 843 (86.9 percent) of the slaves were between the ages of ten and twenty-four, the most marketable years.

TABLE 26. Age Distribution of 93 Slaves on the
Margarita, 1734

Age	Male	Female	Total
10	0	2	2
11	1	2	3
12	22	17	39
13	5	5	10
14	15	0	15
15	2	3	5
16	7	2	9
17	7	0	7
18	1	0	1
Unknown	2	0	2
Total	62	31	93

SOURCE: AGI, Indiferente, 2817.

TABLE 27. Age and Sex of 970 Slaves Imported into Spanish America, 1715–35

Age	Male	Female	Total	Percentage
5–9	17	22	39	4.0
10–14	201	88	289	29.8
15–19	131	146	277	28.6
20–24	177	100	277	28.6
25–29	37	21	58	6.0
30–34	14	9	23	2.4
35–39	4	0	4	0.4
40–50	3	0	3	0.3
Total	584	386	970	100.0

SOURCE: AGI, Contaduría 267, ramos 1–6; Indiferente, 2817.

Only 4 percent of these slaves were under ten. In contrast, Klein has found that during the eighteenth century children in that age group comprised 24 percent of the slaves that went to Cuba and 30 percent of those that arrived between 1815 and 1818.[14]

It is not surprising that the slave's age and sex were the principal determinants of his market value. Prices varied, of course, from time to time and place to place, but it is possible to extract from the records some idea of the magnitude of the purchaser's investment when he bought from the companies. The average price in Jamaica between 1650 and 1688 was £13 1s. 9d., but during the years 1698–1707 the price increased to £19. After the asiento was awarded to England and the trade to Spanish America developed, Jamaican prices jumped to between £20 and £30 per slave. These dramatic increases were sustained for the period 1714–19; thereafter, prices stabilized at between £20 and £25 for a slave in good condition.[15]

The price of a slave delivered to a Spanish American port was much higher. As shown in Table 28, the average annual prices for the years 1715–19 ranged from a low of £33 at Cartagena in 1716 to a high of £60 at Havana in the same year.[16] Unfortunately, information for the 1720s

TABLE 28. Average Prices of Slaves at the Factories, 1715–19

Year	Factory	Number of Slaves in Sample	Average Price (pesos)*	Average Price (£ s. d.)*
1715	Buenos Aires	241	191	43
	Cartagena	337	193	43
1716	Buenos Aires	890	176	40
	Cartagena	156	145	33
	Porto Bello and Panama	630	226	51
	Vera Cruz	114	182	41
	Santiago de Cuba	41	239	54
	Havana	205	266	60
1717	Buenos Aires	264	186	42
	Cartagena	113	152	34
	Porto Bello and Panama	1,084	233	52
	Vera Cruz	280	203	46
	Santiago de Cuba	16	215	48
	Havana	267	248	56
1718	Buenos Aires	1,443	208	47
	Cartagena	243	188	42
	Porto Bello and Panama	1,398	252	57
	Santiago de Cuba	345	203	46
	Havana	407	214	48
1719	Buenos Aires	197	189	43
	Cartagena	294	207	47

SOURCE: AGI, Indiferente, 2847; Contaduría 267, ramos 1–6.

*Prices have been rounded.

TABLE 29. South Sea Company's Estimate for the Average Price of Slaves, 1733

Market	Average Price (pesos)	Average Price (£ s. d.)
Panama and Porto Bello	250	56 5. 0.
Cartagena	220	49 10. 0.
Havana	250	56 5. 0.
Caracas	250	56 5. 0.
Vera Cruz	220	49 10. 0.
Buenos Aires	250	56 5. 0.
Santiago de Cuba	240	54 0. 0.
Santo Domingo	250	56 5. 0.
Trinidad	250	56 5. 0.
Comeagua [Comayagua]*	250	56 5. 0.

SOURCE: Shelburne MSS, vol. 43, 144.
* Mining area in Honduras.

and 1730s is scanty. Scattered evidence suggests, however, that during those years slave prices steadily increased. It appears that by the mid-1730s choice slaves were sold at prices ranging from 230 pesos (£51 15s.) to 270 pesos (£60 15s.) each.

One indication of the average selling price of slaves at the various markets comes from an estimate that the South Sea Company prepared in 1733. As Table 29 shows, there was comparatively slight variation in the price levels at the various markets, and their relative positions seem consistent with the early period, with Cartagena having the lowest prices. The company's estimate should have been reasonably accurate; it was based on at least nineteen years of experience (1714–33) in the slave trade.

That age, sex, and physical attributes affected the price of a slave is amply demonstrated in a list prepared by James Moriarty, a factor at Río de la Hacha in 1727. Moriarty's list, which tabulates both an asking and a selling price, shows something of the bargaining between buyer and seller (see Table 30).

Although the company sold slaves to any customer, however small the purchase, it really preferred to deal with local Spanish middlemen who bought slaves in large lots. As early as 1716 the court of directors told the factors at Panama that it was "better to sell in parcels, though at a price somewhat lower than to sell by retail, or keep them in hopes of better prices." This was sound advice. The price discount to the large-scale deal-

TABLE 30. Description and Prices of Slaves at Río de la Hacha, 1727

Name	Age	Description	Asking Price (pesos)	Selling Price (pesos)
Sammy	22 or 23	A fine negro without blemish	285	275
Antonio	23 or 24	A fine negro	285	275
George	22 or 23	A dull, lazy negro	270	265
Peter	26 or 27	A good negro	280	270
David	18 or 19	A fine negro	265	260
Curacao	17 or 18	Magre [meager] and dronish	250	240
Harry	17 or 18	A good house negro	250	240
Richard	30 or 32	Magre, sick and ugly	255	250
Sambo	13	A good boy	230	220
Miguel	13	A good boy but magre	225	215
Manuel	12 or 13	A fine boy	210	200
Jack	11–12	A fine boy	190	180
Dragle	10–11	A fine boy	190	170
Jeremy	11 or 12	A fine boy but of small growth	180	170
Pancho	9 or 10	Ill featured, recovered of sickness	180	165
Pascual	10 or 11	A fine boy	190	180
Cupido	12 or 13	A fine boy but sore eyes	230	220
Margarita	17 or 18	Full of distempers	260	245
Cecilia	18	A good slave but ugly	270	260
Mary	16 or 17	A fine slave but sick	265	250
Scabby	14 or 15	Scurfed and magre	240	230
Ginny	14 or 15	Lately lost one eye	170	160
Rita	12	A fine girl	190	180
Maria	12	A fine girl	175	165

SOURCE: AGI, Indiferente, 2808.

ers was more than balanced in the company's books by lower overhead in slave maintenance. As the company patiently explained to the Vera Cruz agents in 1716, "Do not keep them in expectation of raising the prices, for you will consider the charge of subsisting them and the great mortality that generally attends them will soon not only eat out the profit but even the prime cost of them, therefore always sell them as soon after arrival as you can."[17]

The company's preference for disposing of large parcels at one time led it to discourage small-scale trade. Writing to the factors at Buenos

Aires in 1723, for example, the court of directors doubted the wisdom "of allowing towne people 15 days to supply themselves with single negroes or small parcels before you sell in large ones." The court of directors reasoned that this practice might make the large-scale dealers feel that they were receiving only the second-best, picked-over slaves. Obviously, such a perception by the big customers would bode ill for the company's ability to retain their patronage.

Sometimes a cargo of apparently desirable slaves was sold at prices far below the company's expectations, which often led the factors to cite the "badness" of the slaves as an excuse. Frequently this explanation was valid, but there were times when it was not. On several occasions the company suspected its employees of having accepted bribes from the Spaniards in return for selling the slaves at a reduced price. In 1723, for example, the factors at Porto Bello complained about the poor quality of two recently arrived cargoes which they had sold cheaply. As it happened, the agents at Jamaica had sent the court of directors depositions swearing to the "goodness" of the same slaves. An indignant reply informed the Porto Bello agents that the company regarded their complaints as "strong proofs of your insincerity and that the dismal condition you give of them is only a plausible reason for your selling or pretending to sell them at such notorious low prices as 200 or 215 pieces of eight [pesos] and at 12 months credit." [18]

The twelve months' credit mentioned in the Porto Bello incident may have been the feature that especially aroused the company's anger. The court of directors always looked askance at granting credit to the Spaniards. As early as 1717 the factors at Vera Cruz were admonished to "sell slaves for ready money . . . we are inclined to ask for cash . . . if it is absolutely necessary to grant credit, enquire about the ability and honesty of such persons, take good security and be cautious." [19] The court of directors was right to be skeptical; it was difficult enough to collect the debts in the best of times, and the periodic outbreaks of war between Britain and Spain virtually wiped the books clean with distressing frequency. [20]

No matter what the company liked or disliked, the agents sometimes could not sell slaves without extending credit to the buyers. Slaves were costly. Most Spaniards bought one, two, or three at a time; very few except the wealthy could afford more than six. Owners of great estates, unless they were very wealthy, went into debt to obtain their labor force. For instance, in 1723 Lady Casablanca bought one hundred slaves on credit to cultivate her "considerable estate" at Lima, contracting on the most favorable terms to repay the debt within four years at 5 percent interest. She was "a particular friend of the new Viceroy," pleaded the factors who had negotiated the sale. They confessed to the company that they had "obliged" the viceroy "in this affair."[21]

Over the years many Spaniards accumulated heavy debts to the South Sea Company. Many simply could not pay, and many others nonchalantly reneged on their obligations. In 1732 the court of directors rather desperately hoped it could collect the "present debts due and outstanding, and payment for their negroes in ready money thereafter, sales upon trust being found by fatal experience too hazardous."[22] But apparently nothing could stop the drain; the company's records reveal that between January 1, 1731, and May 1, 1736, Spanish colonists accumulated a debt of 767,500 pesos (£172,688). Much if not most of this money was lost, since the War of Jenkins' Ear broke out in 1739 and demolished the asiento trade. Table 31 shows the amount of money that was owed to the South Sea Company at each market in 1736.

Spaniards who lacked ready cash had the option of pledging their crops or "fruits of the country" in return for slaves. The English traders accepted sugar, hides, cocoa, tobacco, and logwood as payment. As late as 1736 the company calculated that all the slaves it expected to send annually to Cuba (800) and to Venezuela (500) would be exchanged for "fruits" (sugar and snuff in the case of Cuba, cocoa in the case of Venezuela). For Buenos Aires and Santo Domingo, the court of directors estimated that one-half of the slaves would be paid for in hides. Campeche obtained most of its slaves by exchanging logwood for them; of 151 slaves sold there between 1730 and 1733, only five were bought for cash. The

TABLE 31. Amounts Owing to the South Sea Company, 1736

Market	Owed (pesos)	Owed (£ s. d.)
Panama and Porto Bello	356,000	80,100
Cartagena	20,000	4,500
Havana	100,000	22,500
Santiago de Cuba	33,000	7,425
Vera Cruz	6,000	1,350
Buenos Aires	252,500	56,813
Total	767,500	172,688

SOURCE: Shelburne MSS, vol. 43, 428–29.

company made a few gestures at discontinuing the practice of exchanging slaves for the "fruits of the country" in late 1734, but this policy was never seriously adhered to.[23] Money was in short supply and all efforts to operate solely on a cash basis ultimately failed.

Understandably, the South Sea Company was quite upset at its inability to collect its debts and at the frequently high mortality rate of its slaves in Spanish America. Yet there was little the court of directors could do to alleviate either problem. The granting of credit was indispensable for the conduct of the trade. Slaves fell victim to new diseases or failed to recover from those brought from Africa or contracted during the Atlantic passage. Losses resulting from bad debts and disease were integral parts of the slave trade, and traders had to accept these drawbacks to business as best they could.

NOTES

1. Since most African slaves would already have had some immunity to tropical diseases like malaria and yellow fever, proportionately fewer would die from these causes than would Europeans. To some extent, however, the New World was a new disease environment for the slaves and, as Curtin notes, "everyone in the Americas, or who came to the Americas, paid a price in increased death rates for his entry into this newly created disease environment." See Philip Curtin, "Epidemiology and the Slave Trade," *Political Science Quarterly* 83, no. 2 (June, 1968), 200.

2. Shelburne MSS, vol. 43, 133; vol. 44, 645, 635.

3. Shelburne MSS, vol. 44, 637, 635.

4. Shelburne MSS, vol. 43, 133; vol. 44, 793.

5. Shelburne MSS, vol. 44, 793.

6. Shelburne MSS, vol. 44, 661, 617–23; vol. 43, 133. It is not clear why the incidence of smallpox was higher on Barbados than on the other islands.

7. It should be added that two of these slaves suffered from more than one disorder. For an excellent discussion of the health problems of the slaves at New Granada, see David Lee Chandler, "Health and Slavery: A Study of Health Conditions among Negro Slaves in the Viceroyalty of New Granada and Its Associated Slave Trade, 1600–1810" (Ph.D. thesis, Tulane University, 1972), pp. 176–230.

8. One of the most striking aspects of the table is that the majority of the ships brought their slaves from Angola. As I speculated earlier (see Chapter 2), this was probably due to local preferences for such slaves or to favorable supply conditions in Angola.

9. In a few instances the agents gave an incorrect year for a ship's arrival. I made the appropriate adjustments, using the official shipping records as guides.

10. Shelburne MSS, vol. 44, 542; Palacios Preciado, *La trata de negros*, p. 264.

11. Shelburne MSS, vol. 44, 633, 631–32, 617–23.

12. See AGI, Indiferente, 2817, and Contaduría 267 for ages of slave cargoes.

13. These data were tabulated from the records of the various slave cargoes that listed the ages of the slaves.

14. There is as yet no satisfactory explanation as to why the Cubans received such a high proportion of children in those years. It may well have been the result of Cuban demand as well as of African supply patterns. In comparison to the Cuban example, Klein notes that children under ten comprised only 3 percent of the slaves shipped from Benguela between 1738 and 1784 and 6 percent of those leaving Luanda between 1734 and 1769. See Klein, *Middle Passage*, p. 242.

15. PRO, T70/175, pp. 7, 14.

16. For some factories it was possible to obtain data on the prices of slaves for the five years that were examined. In other cases data were available for only certain years. In the majority of cases discussed, the number of slaves in the sample comprised more than 80 percent of those delivered at the factory during the relevant year. In no case did the sample represent less than 50 percent of the slaves that arrived at the factory during that year.

17. In 1717 the company told its Vera Cruz factors to "try to get contracts for a considerable number of slaves to be taken on arrival . . . you are always to endeavour to sell whole cargoes of negroes from time to time"; see BM, 25563, pp. 18, 7–8, 57–58.

18. BM, 25564, p. 15.

19. BM, 25563, p. 57.

20. In 1717 the court of directors reminded its Vera Cruz factors that "in case of cash, we are more secure in time of war." It was also not unusual for the company to challenge the terms under which its agents granted credit. In 1717, for example, the company was not pleased when the Buenos Aires factors extended twenty months' credit to purchasers of slaves. Observing that twenty months was "very long credit," the court of directors told its men to "avoid this for the future, a negro sold on trust for 20 months is worth 40 pieces of eight [pesos] more than if sold for present money." See BM, 25563, p. 57; 25563, pp. 138–39.

21. BM, 25564, p. 15; 25566, p. 74.

22. BM, 32777, p. 45.

23. Shelburne MSS, vol. 43, 44, 267; BM, 25552, p. 8.

8 Stresses and Strains, 1714–39

In the century and a half before the Treaty of Utrecht the English and the Spanish had built up a tradition of mutual antipathy. Countless conflicts, intermittent warfare, economic and imperial rivalry, and religious hostility left a heritage of chauvinism and intolerance on both sides. Such passions continued unabated throughout the period between 1714 and 1739. Relations between the South Sea Company and the Spanish were prickly in the best periods and bitterly hostile in the worst. It is difficult to find a single part of the asiento trade that functioned smoothly. The Spanish believed the company used its contractual privileges as a cover for contraband trade, and they were right. The company accused the Spaniards of venality and obstructionism, and the charges were amply justified.

One of the company's grievances was the imposition of unauthorized taxes, duties, and charges by local officials in Spanish America. In 1717, for example, the officials at Panama required the residents to pay a tax of 2.5 percent of the value of each slave they purchased. The following year the officials in Peru ordered the buyers to pay a 4-peso tax on every slave purchase. The authorities in Spain admitted that these levies were illegal, but they continued to be reintroduced at regular intervals. In 1735 the royal officials at Buenos Aires set a charge of 15 pesos on each slave that was bought and taken into the interior provinces. Similarly, each slave purchase was subject to a tax of 16 pesos at Potosí (Peru) and 4 pesos at Santiago (Chile). The court of directors estimated that the total illegal tax paid on each slave bought at Buenos Aires and taken to Peru or Chile amounted to 50 to 60 pesos.[1]

The company argued persuasively that these burdensome taxes were harmful to business. Protesting the exactions at Buenos Aires, the court of directors labeled them "doubly prejudicial" because they increased "the price of the slaves which lessens the sales in small parcels and encourages illicit trade with the Portuguese." The Junta de Negros in Madrid agreed and ordered the charges removed.[2]

The company was billed for services that should have been rendered free of charge. In 1718 the clergy at Panama demanded that the English pay a fee of 6 pesos 3 reales (£2 9s.) for each company slave whose funeral service they conducted. A few years later the agents at Panama had to pay the medical inspector 165 pesos for visiting three slave ships. The Junta de Negros ordered the money refunded after the company protested. In 1735 the officials at Porto Bello imposed a fee of 12 pesos for regulating each cargo of arriving slaves.[3]

The list of obnoxious special charges seemed endless. The company objected strongly to a 3-peso duty levied on each slave indulted in Panama in 1717. This measure seems to have been rescinded later by the authorities in Madrid. When the Panamanian officials attempted to extract 3 pesos per slave introduced there in 1735, the court of directors immediately protested that it was already required to pay an import duty of 33⅓ pesos on each pieza under the asiento. The records do not reveal how this dispute was resolved.[4]

On at least two occasions the company protested against port charges levied on its ships at Buenos Aires. In 1718 the court of directors complained to the British government about the "exorbitant" charges, submitting six ships' records as evidence (see Table 32). In later years excessive port charges were not mentioned, so presumably the problem was resolved. The court of directors did report in 1735 that the agents at Buenos Aires had been forced to pay 1,080 pesos (£243) for "pilotage of ships," a service that the agents said "was never performed."[5]

Article 9 of the asiento contract created a festering grievance at Buenos Aires. The article provided that the English should receive lands adjacent to the city on which to cultivate crops and breed cattle for themselves and the slaves. No such land was assigned, however, and the Spanish crown issued a cédula in October, 1716, in response to company complaints, ordering that the contract be upheld. The royal officials announced that the king had no lands near the city that were suitable for the purpose. The company then demanded "a reasonable satisfaction for the damages they sustain and the charges they are put to for want of such lands." Neither lands nor compensation was ever received, and the South Sea Company brooded for years over the Spaniards' duplicity.[6]

TABLE 32. Port Charges on Six Company Ships at Buenos Aires, 1715–18

Ship	Tonnage	Port Charges (pesos)	Port Charges (£ s. d.)
Indian Queen	220	889	200
Europe	300	957	215
Wiltshire	142	923	208
Prince of Wales	260	889	200
Windsor	240	1,363	307
Warwick	?	1,612	363

SOURCE: BM, 25555, p. 90.

There were other irritations to contend with. In 1716 the company objected to unauthorized Spanish officials sending guards aboard the slave ships at the ports. Article 22 of the asiento had given the royal officials the right to appoint guards to search and inspect ships in port, but unauthorized persons had arrogated to themselves this right, and the company resented the resulting confusion and the cost of feeding the guards. Quite possibly the English were more upset by the fact that the presence of guards inhibited the conduct of the contraband trade. In any case the Spanish crown issued a cédula in November, 1716, ordering its officials to abide by the terms of the contract. The cédula was effective temporarily, but by 1728 the company was again outraged by searches of ships made "in a very insolent manner" by unauthorized persons.[7]

The company was equally irked in 1718 when the royal officials at Panama insisted on being a party to all the business negotiations between the agents and their customers and wanted to "assist in receiving all merchandise and negroes." And it objected in 1728 when the officials at Peru demanded to be present at business transactions between the English and the local residents. The court of directors hinted that this was "being done with a view to embarrass and obstruct the Company's affairs." Probably the officials at Panama and Peru hoped that their presence during the company's business negotiations might deter illegal trading. It seems a safe guess that the intrusions ceased once the Spaniards assured themselves that the illicit trade was under control or after the English gave them appropriate regalos.[8]

A much more serious dispute broke out in Peru about 1730. The viceroy, in a blatant attempt to harass the English, forbade the Peruvians to take any money to Porto Bello or Panama except during the annual trade fair. His order would force the company to sell its slaves on credit and wait until the fair to be paid. The agents viewed this prospect with alarm, having already had difficulty in collecting debts from the Spaniards. This measure was apparently never stringently enforced, but neither was it abrogated. Perhaps it was merely a feint to keep the company off balance. Peruvian bureaucrats seem to have enjoyed the game; in 1735 the company was complaining that "the ports of Peru have of late years often been shut by the Spanish Governors for a considerable time to our very great prejudice as thereby the necessary moneys for the purchase of our negroes, and payment of the debts due to us have been stopped."[9]

One complaint made by the company, but more frequently and vociferously by English private traders, was that their ships were being chased and attacked by Spanish pirates. The Caribbean Sea had long been infested by pirates, who operated with impunity principally from Puerto Rico. These raids were winked at or even actively supported by the Spanish. In 1727 some English traders obtained possession of a letter allegedly written to the leading officials in the Americas by Joseph Patiño, Secretary of State for Marine and the Indies. The letter said, "His Majesty is resolved that in the American seas cruising [or privateering] be executed against all . . . the subjects of the English, and in consequence thereof His Majesty commands that you permit and persuade all his vassals that are so disposed to arm and fitt out cruisers [or privateers] that they may do it freely and without any embarrassment whatsoever against the subjects of the said English nation."[10]

It is quite possible that the letter was genuine. Certainly the reported incidents of piracy increased in the 1730s, and the patriotic fervor aroused by such attacks would contribute to the outbreak of the War of Jenkins' Ear. Among the more notorious pirates was Miguel Enríquez, who made his headquarters in Puerto Rico. Agent Jonathan Dennis reported from Cuba in 1731 that Enríquez and his one hundred followers preyed on French and English shipping "using the people with the greatest cruelty"; Enríquez put some of his victims "on shoar, on what we call a moroond [marooned] island, that is an uninhabitable place to perish in." Dennis characterized the pirates as "the most abominable robbers of mankind."[11]

The attacks on English traders exacerbated relations between the two nations, but it may be doubted whether they seriously affected the company's physical ability to fulfill its contractual obligations. In any case, the presence of outlaws on the high seas and the failure of the Spanish government to curb their depredations allowed the company to question whether the Spaniards were seriously interested in the fulfillment of the asiento contract.

In addition to the harassment by pirates, there were reports that Englishmen were being mistreated in Spanish American ports. In 1727 it was said that James Moriarty, a company agent, had been held prisoner at Santa Marta and "loaded with irons." Although he was not formally charged, officials confiscated his sloop, possessions, and clothing and temporarily imprisoned his crew. A few years later the company charged that some of its sailors had been "cruelly and inhumanly treated in their persons in so much that several have lost their lives and many narrowly escaped." The court of directors did not cite specific instances of such abuse in this particular statement, but it would not be surprising if such cases did occur.[12]

The adjudication of disputes with the Spaniards merely confirmed the South Sea Company's sense of grievance and injustice. The judges conservators, who had sole jurisdiction over local disputes arising from the asiento, seldom commanded the company's respect. The court of directors accused them of partisanship, pointing out that "when suits are brought against the estate of debtors for the collection of unpaid money on slaves, the suits are unfairly adjudicated." The judges conservators were "of little service and oftentimes oppressors instead of protectors of the Company's privileges." The company also alleged that, in violation of Article 13 of the asiento contract, other tribunals insisted on hearing cases involving the company; consequently "the Judge Conservator's power is almost wholly annihilated, though the Company at the same time pays them very considerable salarys."[13]

Still another exasperating nuisance was the scarcity of notaries in the Indies to record the agents' complaints. Even the few available were wholly unethical, according to the company. In April, 1735, the agents at Cartagena reported that when "we talk of complaining to the Company," the royal officials "laugh at us for as the escribano [notary] is one of the set, they know he will not give any authentic testimony of their proceedings." Several months later the court of directors informed Ambassador Keene in Madrid that the notaries were "absolutely in the Governors' power, being obliged to wait the Governors' and royal officers' leave whereby authentic testimonys are withheld till the ships are sailed which should carry them home." The company's request for correction of this abuse seems not to have elicited any action by the Spanish government; there is no evidence that the government was even interested in the matter.[14]

Many of the disputes discussed thus far were peripheral to the asiento trade, but the principal provisions of the treaty caused difficulties too. These disputes not only centered on matters relating to the supply of slaves but on problems concerning the annual ship. It may be recalled that the South Sea Company had the right to send a special ship laden with consumer goods to be sold at the annual fair. The new convention of 1716 stipulated that the company should be told in advance when and where the fair would be held, but this was not always done, much to the chagrin of the court of directors. In 1718 the Spaniards refused to issue the company's license to send the annual ship, claiming that the markets in the Americas were oversupplied with consumer goods. Naturally the company was indignant, particularly since the notification came after it had purchased £300,000 worth of cargo. In 1724 the crown again prohibited the sending of a ship to the fair, giving the same excuse of oversupply. Owing to the crown's various refusals to grant licenses and the interruptions of trade during the two wars (1719–21 and 1727–29), the company sent only eight annual ships to the Americas in the twenty-five years of the asiento. The last and most profitable voyage was made in 1732.[15]

The Spanish crown's refusal to grant licenses had some justification. The royal officials had amassed evidence that the company's contraband trade had introduced more commodities than would legally have been permitted under the terms of the contract. Since the annual ship was believed to be the company's most profitable venture, the crown retaliated by canceling it. A company contract violation would be balanced by an illegality on the part of the Spaniards. This issue, probably more than any other, generated so much ill will and so poisoned relations between the two parties that negotiation in good faith became virtually impossible.[16]

The slave trade provisions of the asiento also produced their share of heated controversy between the company and the Spaniards. From an early date the crown and some of the colonists disparaged the company for failing to supply the 4,800 piezas per year required by the contract. While the crown asserted that the company was more interested in supplying the Americas with commodities other than slaves, some colonists— the Cubans, for instance—complained that the shortage of slaves had obliged them to abandon the sugar industry. The company's sensitivity to these criticisms perhaps betrayed a guilty conscience. It hotly denied that the slave trade had been superseded by the trade in textiles and other consumer goods, and insisted that it was "supplying the number of negroes the market was capable of taking off."[17]

The company's protestations of innocence were not convincing. The court of directors worried less about the slave trade and the fulfillment of its contractual obligations in that area and more about the annual ship, the commodities for the Spanish market, and the kind and extent of the returns from Spanish America. These returns, which were sold in Europe at a profit, included indigo, logwood, and cochineal from Mexico, sugar from Cuba, hides from Buenos Aires, and cocoa from Venezuela. Silver, of course, was also highly desirable.

The slave trade both facilitated and gave a cloak of legitimacy to other types of commerce. The asiento contract allowed the company the privilege of sending each year a ship of 150 tons' burden with supplies for the factories. This vessel, not to be confused with the annual ship sent to the fair, invariably carried goods ostensibly for the use of the factories but in fact sold clandestinely to the colonists. On the pretext of provisioning the slaves, many slave ships brought goods intended for sale to the colonists. A familiar tactic to advance the illicit commerce was to put a few slaves (often ten or less) on board a vessel to "qualify" it as engaged in the asiento trade, thereby assuring its admission to a Spanish port. After disposing of its cargo of slaves and perhaps selling some flour or other goods, the vessel would be laden with Spanish commodities purchased with the proceeds from the sale of the slaves and the contraband goods.

Once the Spanish crown became aware of these deceptions, it endeavored to prevent them. It accused the company of being involved in illicit trade and at the same time appealed for aid in stopping it. The company consistently denied any knowledge of or participation in illegal commerce but did concede in 1728 that if such trade existed, it was with the connivance of the royal officials. In the following year, however, the court of directors tacitly recognized that some of its employees were engaged in contraband trade; one of its committees was asked to "consider the most effectual methods and means" for its prevention.[18]

The illegal trade was not altogether the preserve of the lower-ranking employees; officers of the company, including the governor, sent their own illegal trade goods aboard the company's slave ships. In 1725 the Spanish officers at Buenos Aires intercepted a very discreet letter from the factors to the subgovernor and deputy governor of the company, informing them that a quantity of silver was being forwarded to London on the *Sea Horse* "on the account of the secret commerce."[19]

Hard evidence notwithstanding, the court of directors brazenly continued to deny any connection with the illegal trade. A letter of 1732 to the duke of Newcastle professed ignorance of the matter and challenged the Spaniards to prove their accusations of company complicity and "say by whom, when, upon what ships, in what instance, and that they not only allege but prove the fact." This assertion of innocence was for the consumption of English officials, since the company realized that the Spanish accusations did have some basis in fact. Over the years Spanish officials had found illicit goods in several company ships, chiefly at Panama, Buenos Aires, and Havana.[20]

When the company failed to take effective steps to curb the contraband trade, the angry Spaniards retaliated by harassing English ships. Several were detained in port on the charge, often spurious, that they were engaged in the illicit trade. Between 1730 and 1734 at least twelve ships were held for varying periods of time, some as long as a year. The Spaniards also undertook, with some success, an aggressive campaign to search all arriving company ships for illicit cargo. Several cargoes were seized, including two that had been dispatched by agents Rigby and Pratter from Jamaica. To save face, the embarrassed company relieved Rigby of his duties, but Pratter died before he could be reprimanded or punished.[21]

To stop the abuses in the asiento trade, the Spaniards issued a number of regulations in 1733. Thomas Geraldino, the Spanish agent in London, ordered in the king's name that all provisions carried by the slave ships for the use of the slaves should be secured in magazines having three different locks. The keys to two of the locks would be held by two different royal officials; the third key would be kept by a company agent. By this means, the cooperation of three men would be necessary before such commodities could be sold clandestinely. Geraldino emphasized that "no commerce may be carried on with the surplus as hitherto has been most notoriously practised." The company eventually objected to Spanish officials possessing keys to its stores, but there is no evidence that the order was either rescinded or consistently implemented.[22]

Geraldino also tried to end the company's practice of "qualifying" ships by putting a few slaves on board. He ordered the royal officials to refuse entry to vessels that did not have a "complete loading." Geraldino defined "complete loading" as a ratio of four slaves to every five tons of a ship's burden; thus a ship weighing one hundred tons was supposed to carry eighty slaves. No vessel was exempt unless the company procured a special certificate of dispensation. In a related matter Geraldino instructed the royal officials "not to permit anything to be put on board the vessels employed by the Company but what shall appear to be the produce of the slaves introduced by them." The company later gave assurance that it would cooperate with these policies.[23]

There is little doubt that the Spanish government was serious in attacking the abuses of the asiento trade. Enforcement, however, depended upon the honesty, energy, and efficiency of the royal officials in the colonies. How successful they were is difficult to estimate. Clearly, the question of contraband trade was a bitterly divisive issue between the company and the Spanish crown. The South Sea Company was certainly eager to see the illegal trade by competing interlopers stopped, but it was just as eager to continue its own. Perhaps this ambivalence, together with its usual pose of injured innocence, accounted for the unusual truculence of a 1732 pronouncement:

> Were the government of Spain in the Indies, as vigilant against the contraband trade introduc'd and transacted there, as the Company is to prevent it here, and would they who have it in their power, put in execution with as much severity as the Company wishes, the authoritys of the treatys by seizing and conficating all unlawful imports and exports, there would be no want of confidence, no jealousys or uneasiness on either side, nor any want of compliance here, in everything that could be reasonably ask'd. But hard is and will be the fate of the Company, and all Asientists, if the defects and imperfections of the Spanish government are to be laid to the door of the contractors with them.[24]

Spain's unhappiness was manifested in the crude, often unnecessary obstacles it placed in the company's path. At times the Spaniards apparently wanted to provoke the British government and the company into a voluntary abrogation of the contract. The company's assertion in 1730 that it observed in the Spanish crown "not only a disposition . . . to refuse any reasonable favours, but to put every art in practice in order to the ruin and destruction of the commerce of the Asiento" was not only perceptive but substantially correct.[25]

One seemingly unnecessary conflict that the crown gratuitously engineered concerned the sale to the Spanish colonists of slaves who had spent some time in the British islands. For many years the company had landed slaves in Jamaica and Barbados for "refreshment" prior to sending them to Spanish America. It also bought a sizable proportion of its slaves in those two islands to complete its cargoes. No objection was raised to this practice until October, 1724, when the Spanish crown abruptly ordered the officials not to admit any slaves who had been in the British colonies; in the future the slaves were to come directly from Africa.[26]

The ostensible reason for this decision was that the slaves were being tainted with heresy in the British colonies, thereby making their conversion to Roman Catholicism more difficult. The company protested that the order was contrary to the spirit of the asiento and was "equal to, if not worse than an abolition of the treaty." The slaves had to be refreshed before being shipped to Spanish America; besides, the stopover enabled the agents to assemble cargoes of "none but what are sound and healthy and of proper sorts" for the Spanish markets. The Spanish crown's order was "inhumane to the negroes, and destructive to the Company's interest . . . and pernicious to His Majesty's subjects." The company spurned the religious argument as specious: the Spaniards "cannot be so stupid" as to believe "that removing the negroes from one vessel to another, or giving them a few days refreshment . . . would instil heretical principles in them."[27]

In deference to the company's strong reaction, the crown proposed a slight modification: it would permit the entry into Spanish America of slaves who had spent no longer than thirty days in a British colony. The court of directors renounced this compromise, partly because "it put us under a restraint not stipulated by the treatys." Years of acrimonious dealings with the Spaniards had convinced the company not to accept a proposal which had the potential for producing another interminable series of squabbles. In this instance the court of directors was sure that there would be rancorous disputes over the length of time the slaves had stayed in the islands. The British minister in Madrid was informed that it would be "very difficult if not impracticable to send with the negroes such vouchers as would convince the scrupulous Spaniards, especially if they were disposed to be refractory, that the negroes had not been in Jamaica beyond the time limit."[28]

The matter was resolved, at least temporarily, in July, 1725, when the king issued a cédula admitting slaves who had been in the British colonies no more than four months. The traders were required to submit documents attesting to the length of each slave's sojourn in the islands. Although the company would have preferred no time restrictions, it was prepared to accept this latest offer as an acceptable compromise. However, the crown was enjoying itself at the company's expense, for in December, 1726, a new cédula reinstated the ban against slaves who had spent any time whatsoever in the British colonies. The weary routine of charges and countercharges went on.[29] None of these cédulas made any real difference to the trade, since the crown had never seriously intended to enforce them. They were merely moves in a cat-and-mouse game with the company. But the game consumed the energies of both protagonists with no result other than bruised feelings and mutual weariness.

Another bit of mock warfare was fought over the residence of company agents at Panama. At the outset of the asiento trade the company had established a factory at Panama and a subsidiary one at Porto Bello. The contract allowed factors to live at the ports but not in the interior areas or "inland countrys." On December 8, 1726, the crown suddenly announced that Panama was not a port but an inland area and hence was debarred as a place of residence for the agents. Once the company recovered from the shock, it issued a strong protest, noting that Panama was "notoriously known to be one of the greatest ports in the South Seas." In addition, the cédula was "not only contrary to the eleventh article of the Asiento which gives the Company leave to settle factorys at all parts of America without distinction but is contrary to the practice of all former Asientists and inconsistent with the tenth article of the Asiento contract which has included Panama by name among the ports which the Company may make use of for shipping their negroes for Peru."[30]

The squabble dragged on interminably, with the South Sea Company's agents remaining at Panama but always under the threat of expulsion. Finally, in December, 1731, the local officials ordered the agents to leave within fifteen days, and this time they meant it. The English retired to Porto Bello, a settlement the company had described as "the most unhealthy place in the world." The company was now more determined than ever to get the original cédula rescinded. In 1733 the British ambassador to Madrid was urged to direct "your particular attention to the affair of the Company's right to the residence of their factory at Panama, which we cannot on any occasion give up."[31]

Whether this problem was ever resolved is not clear; a cédula dated April 13, 1734, permitted the agents to return temporarily to Panama but gave the local authorities the right to decide whether their residence there was necessary for the conduct of the company's business. The records are silent from this point on, but it makes little difference; the Spanish government had achieved its purpose of teasing the company into impotent rage.[32]

Another tiresome controversy began when Spain seized a quantity of the company's merchandise, money, and slaves during the wars with England in 1719–21 and 1727–29. In neither case did Spain give the company the eighteen-month grace period to remove its possessions as required by Article 40 of the contract. After the wars ended, the crown ordered the confiscated property returned, but the company lost heavily in the process. For one thing, the royal officials had already spent some of the confiscated funds, which they were unable or unwilling to replace. For another, the parties could not agree on the value of the confiscated property. The Spaniards finally admitted in 1735 that they owed the company 1,500,000 pesos (£337,500), but the court of directors insisted that its records showed "a much greater sum," closer in fact to £1,500,000. The company pressured the Spanish by refusing to pay the customs duties it owed, nor would it pay the 25 percent of the profits for each annual ship, as stipulated in the asiento contract. By 1737 the amount outstanding for duties and for the last annual ship (dispatched in 1732) was £68,000.[33]

Through much of the period the two sides were locked in a currency dispute. Prior to 1726 the company calculated its duties in the *peso escudo de plata*, the coin used in Spain. It was worth about 4s. 6d. in British currency and was eight times the value of the *real de plata*, the coin used in Spanish America. In 1726 the crown devalued the colonial *real de plata*; the peso was now reckoned at ten times the value of the new real. Since the company was paid by the colonists in reales, it insisted on paying its duties to the crown at the old 8 : 1 ratio, while collecting from the customers at 10 : 1. The company contended that the 8 : 1 rate in effect when the treaty was signed in 1713 should not be changed during the life of the asiento. The crown rejected this argument, and neither side showed any disposition to compromise.[34]

These seemingly insoluble problems threatened to bring the asiento trade to a premature halt. In 1732 Geraldino, possibly acting on royal orders, suggest that the company might wish to cancel the contract in return for a cash settlement. The company's attorneys, however, advised that the provisions of a treaty between Spain and England could not be set aside by a private company.[35] In 1734 the company petitioned George II to abrogate the treaty. It is doubtful whether the company expected its request to be taken seriously; rather, it may well have intended the petition to draw the British government into its struggles with the Spanish. But His Majesty's government, under Walpole's leadership, had no taste for unnecessary brawls, and there is no evidence that the subject was revived in later years.[36] For its part, the Spanish crown spent the last five years of the asiento period threatening to end the trade unless the company paid the outstanding duties. This oft-repeated threat was made for the last time just before the outbreak of the War of Jenkins' Ear in 1739.[37]

In the company's considered opinion a cessation of the trade was not the way out of the impasse. In December, 1737, the court of directors informed George II that it wanted to retain the trade for the entire thirty years as awarded by the treaty, and that those years "wherein the Company's trade was obstructed are not to be taken in the account." On the other hand, the Spaniards were anxious by this time to remove the trade from English hands and put it in those of their own countrymen. Ambassador Benjamin Keene reported from Madrid in 1739 that the marquis de Villarias had told him that "there were Spaniards now who had proposals to supply the Indies with negroes, and that they had no occasion for foreign assistance, nor would his Catholic Majesty ever let it go out of the management of such companies of his own subjects as were willing and pressing to enter into a contract." Villarias overstated the Spaniards' ability to supply their whole slave market, but it is true that they handled an increasing proportion of the slave trade to their own colonies as the eighteenth century wore on.[38]

In retrospect it must be said that the slave trade was partly responsible for the mounting ill will and distrust between the English and the Spanish during the 1730s. In addition, the old hatreds complicated the South Sea Company's conduct of the trade and helped to ensure the failure of the asiento. By 1750 both nations accepted the inevitable and abrogated the contract.

NOTES

1. BM, 25555, p. 93; 32788, p. 169; 25563, p. 22; AGI, Indiferente, 2809, 2811.

2. AGI, Indiferente, 2809, 2811.

3. BM, 25555, p. 93; AGI, Indiferente, 2776, 2811; BM, 32788, p. 174.

4. BM, 25563, p. 22.

5. BM, 32788, p. 169.

6. BM, 25555, p. 93; 25553, pp. 13–27.

7. AGI, Indiferente, 2800; BM, 25552, p. 8; 25553, pp. 13–27.

8. BM, 25553, pp. 13–27.

9. BM, 32770, p. 10; 32787, p. 288.

10. Shelburne MSS, vol. 44, 327.

11. Shelburne MSS, vol. 44, 339–53. Dennis's characterization of these pi-

rates was not unique. The court of directors of the South Sea Company even described the Spanish Guarda Costas at Puerto Rico as "an armada of pirates" after they attacked some of the company's vessels. See BM, 32775, p. 14.

12. BM, 25553, p. 8; 33032, p. 43.

13. BM, 32788, p. 169; 25553, pp. 13–27.

14. AGI, Indiferente, 2811; BM, 32788, pp. 250, 169.

15. BM, 25556, p. 34.

16. For an analysis of trade as conducted by the annual ships, see William G. Wood, "The Annual Ships of the South Sea Company" (Ph.D. thesis, University of Illinois, Urbana, 1939).

17. BM, 25563, pp. 196–99, 165–67; 32769, p. 104; 25506, p. 35.

18. BM, 25557, pp. 16–20; 25504, p. 7; 25553, p. 14.

19. AGI, Indiferente, 2785.

20. BM, 32776, p. 44; AGI, Indiferente, 2807, 2804, 2805; Contaduría 268, ramo 1. For discussions of the South Sea Company's contraband trade, see V. L. Brown, "The South Sea Company and Contraband Trade," *American Historical Review* 31, no. 4 (1926), 662–78; and G. H. Nelson, "The Asiento System 1730–39" (Ph.D. thesis, University of Michigan, 1933).

21. BM, 32787, pp. 288–90; 25507, pp. 57–58; 25554, p. 128; 25504, p. 221; 25506, p. 14; AGI, Indiferente, 2811, 2810.

22. BM, 32782, pp. 30, 228.

23. BM, 25506, pp. 148–50; 32782, p. 230; 25577, pp. 74–75; 25554, p. 10.

24. BM, 32776, p. 44.

25. BM, 32770, p. 10.

26. BM, 25556, p. 69.

27. BM, 25553, pp. 13–27.

28. BM, 25564, pp. 113–14.

29. BM, 25553, pp. 13–27.

30. BM, 25553, pp. 13–27; 32784, p. 314; 32782, p. 303.

31. BM, 32776, p. 218; 32784, p. 314; 32782, p. 303.

32. BM, 32784, p. 314; 32788, p. 173.

33. BM, 25561, pp. 104–5; 32787, pp. 288–90; 32800, p. 101; 25545, p. 67.

34. Shelburne MSS, vol. 43, 217–19; BM, 32782, pp. 319–25.

35. BM, 25506, p. 45.

36. Richard Pares, *War and Trade in the West Indies, 1739–1763* (London: Frank Cass & Co., 1963), p. 19. Sperling maintains that the British government feared that if the trade were surrendered, it would be inherited by the French; see *South Sea Company*, p. 45.

37. BM, 25507, p. 149; 32786, p. 348; 32800, p. 103. For discussion of the South Sea Company's role in the outbreak of the War of Jenkins' Ear, see Sperling,

South Sea Company, pp. 45–48; E. G. Hildner, "The Role of the South Sea Company in the Diplomacy Leading to the War of Jenkins' Ear, 1729–1739," *Hispanic American Historical Review* 18, no. 3 (1938), 322–41; and Jean McLachlan, *Trade and Peace with Old Spain*, *1667–1750* (1940; reprinted, New York: Octagon Books, 1974), pp. 78–121.

38. BM, 32799, p. 57; 32800, p. 297.

9 The Profitability of the Trade

In the history of the slave trade the question of profitability is something of a quagmire. Several scholars have suggested that the trade as a whole was immensely rewarding; others have argued that few traders received significant returns on their investment.[1] The records which have survived are invariably incomplete and quite often lack the precise data needed to fit the parts of the puzzle together. Slave trade figures, in addition, are sometimes used selectively, and the records lend themselves to conflicting interpretations. This chapter attempts to describe some aspects of the South Sea Company's finances, although none of these findings should be taken as definitive. On the contrary, they are provisional and are advanced with some trepidation.

The company's records demonstrate that no complete picture of its financial position can be based simply on the costs involved in marketing slaves and the price received from their sale. To mention but one complication, the company's customers paid for many of the slaves in the "fruits of the country," such as cocoa, sugar, and hides. Only if we knew the net income from the resale of these products could we estimate the company's earnings from this aspect of the slave trade. Thus one problem of profitability raises another, one that is anything but easy to resolve.

The company's records are incomplete for some years and missing for others. They do not always clearly distinguish between expenses specifically related to the slave trade and those arising from other aspects of the company's commerce, such as the annual ship. The company did not always know the truth about its operations, and there is reason to believe that sometimes it deliberately misrepresented the state of affairs. The illicit trade in which it habitually engaged only deepens the obscurity of the economic problem. Some items of expenditure and income are hardly measurable from the records but may well have amounted to significant sums; we know, for example, that company employees frequently distributed regalos or bribes to Spanish officials, but to what extent did these modify the profit margin overall or in particular times and places?

A number of accounts of individual slave cargoes have survived, and an examination of the *Sea Nymph*'s delivery of 100 slaves from Barbados to Caracas in 1735 illustrates some of the problems in calculating profit margins in the trade (see Table 33). The *Sea Nymph*'s records itemize the expenditures to the port of Caracas but say nothing about the costs at the factory, which would have been substantial. Port fees, payments to judges conservators and other officials, duty to the crown (which depended on the evaluation of the cargo in piezas), rental for the negrory, maintenance of the slaves until sale, and a host of other expenses are absent from the record. Nothing is known of the amount of cash or "fruits" received from the sale of these 100 slaves. There is little point in trying to ascertain the profit on this particular voyage, although the records do help in estimating the typical costs of delivery up to a point. By comparing many such partial records, we can reach general estimates of the company's expenditures on slave cargoes, as we shall see.[2]

There is little doubt that a large outlay of capital was required for acquiring slaves. If the company fitted out the ship destined for Africa, it was liable for the cost of the charter, the wages of captain and crew, the purchase of the slaves, the cost of insurance, and provisions for everyone on board. Alternatively, the company could agree to buy at a set price in the islands or in Buenos Aires slaves purchased and transported by private traders. The company, of course, would be liable for the various expenses associated with the sale of the slaves in Spanish America—maintenance costs, agents' commissions, physicians' fees, port charges, and so on.

To take care of certain necessary expenses at a factory—food for the slaves, physicians' fees, wages for the supervisors of the captives, and rental of the negrory—the company allowed the agent a drawing account, or "tariff of charges," that set a maximum amount allowable per item. The allowance for some items increased over time; that for other items varied according to the location of the factory. The "tariffs of charges" for the factories at Havana and Santiago de Cuba in 1729 show the kinds of expenses that were incurred in caring for the slaves at the factories. This par-

TABLE 33. Expenditures on 100 Slaves Sent to Caracas, 1735

	£ s. d.
To cost of 12 boys at £22	264 0. 0.
To cost of 88 mostly men boys and women girls at £25 [teen-agers]	2,200 0. 0.
[Sub] Total	2,464 0. 0.
Commission at 5%	123 4. 0.
[Sub] Total	2,587 4. 0.
To maintenance at Barbados till put on board at 5 pence per day	88 14. 6.
To sundry other expenses	17 3. 9.
To provisions put on board for the passage	45 13. 1½.
To 55 jackets and breeches for the boys at 4s. 2d. each	11 9. 2.
To 45 petticoats and westcoats for the girls at 4s. 7d. each	10 6. 3.
[Sub] Total	173 6. 9½.
Commission thereon	8 13. 4.
[Sub] Total	182 0. 1½.
To the amount of sundry stores and necessarys for the sloop, Sea Nymph	177 2. 9.
Commission thereon	8 17. 1½.
[Sub] Total	185 19. 1½.
To hire of sloop from 12 May 1735 to 12 Sept. at £45 per month	180 0. 0.
To sailors' wages	158 10. 6.
Commission thereon	16 18. 6.
[Sub] Total	355 9. 0.
[Total]	£3,310 12. 3.

SOURCE: Shelburne MSS, vol. 43, 127.

ticular estimate, based on a quota of 550 slaves to be sold annually, allowed for:

1. Port charges on five ships to carry the slaves: 231 pesos (£52) each.
2. Provisions for 550 slaves for twelve days: ⅔ real (5d.) per day.
3. Rent of the negrory: 1 peso (4s. 6d.) per slave.

4. A slave keeper, a nurse, and a barber-surgeon (total for the three): 4 reales (1s. 8d.) per slave.

5. Five bomboys [overseers] for Havana and three for Santiago de Cuba: 2-3 real per day.

6. Doctor and medicines: 2 pesos (9s.) per slave.

7. Burial of sixteen slaves who were expected to die: 7 pesos (£1 11s. 6d.) per burial.

8. Petty charges: 1½ pesos (6s. 9d.) per slave.

9. Commission on gross sales: 5 percent.[3]

The first group of records used to estimate the profitability of the trade is the factory returns roughly covering the years 1714–21. Since these records lack one or more of the essential types of information, estimated figures are supplied where necessary. In particular, the costs of delivery and marketing are generally absent. For the purposes of this study, the following standard estimates are made:

1. Four actual slaves equal three piezas in cases where the documents do not record the official valuation.[4]

2. Fifteen percent of the slaves purchased in Africa died in transit, and the average cost of each deceased slave was 63 pesos 4 reales (£14).

3. The cost of purchasing one slave in Jamaica or Barbados, transporting him to any factory in Spanish America, and selling him there was 142 pesos (£32), exclusive of duty to the Spanish crown. (Since the duty actually paid was based on the number of piezas, there is no need to estimate it.)

4. The cost of purchasing one slave in Africa, transporting him directly to any factory in Spanish America, and selling him there was 97 pesos (£22), exclusive of duty.

5. The cost of purchasing one slave in Africa, landing him at Jamaica or Barbados for refreshment, and transporting him to any factory in Spanish America was 107 pesos (£24), exclusive of duty.

6. Slaves who survived the crossing and were landed at a factory in Spanish America, but who died before sale, cost about as much as those who lived to be sold.

The rationale for the estimates given above are found in Appendices 1, 2, and 3.

Bearing in mind that these estimates are only approximations, we can

compute the profitability rate for the factories whose slave trade records
are extant by using the formula

$$P = \frac{a - x}{x} \quad (100)$$

where P is the rate of profitability, a is the receipts from the sale of the
slaves, and x, the total capital investment, is a summation of the purchase,
transportation, and maintenance costs of the slaves who were eventually
sold, the expenditure on those who died in transit, and the duty that was
paid on the piezas.

Table 34 shows the results for Buenos Aires (1714–19), Porto Bello
and Panama (1714–18, 1721), and Cartagena (1714–18). The detailed
findings for these three factories (see Appendices 4–9) demonstrate that
the rate of profitability varied in accordance with where the slaves were
purchased and where they were sold. It ranged from a high of 68.1 percent
for slaves purchased in Africa, refreshed in the islands, and then sold at
Porto Bello and Panama, to a low of 1.6 percent for slaves bought in the
islands and sold at Cartagena. Profits were highest at Porto Bello and Panama, most likely because the greater demand for slaves there caused prices
to rise. The converse was probably true for Cartagena.

Scattered data for the years 1727 and 1730–32 provide some further
indications of the economics of the trade. These data are available for
Buenos Aires, Havana, Porto Bello, and Panama. For Buenos Aires the
data include records for one cargo of slaves that arrived in 1727 and two
that came in 1730; all three ships brought their slaves from Madagascar.
By using the formula

$$P = \frac{a - x}{x} \quad (100)$$

our calculation suggests that the company obtained a profit of 38.0 percent on the 817 slaves which the three ships delivered.[5]

The Panama and Porto Bello records for fifteen cargoes of slaves that
arrived from the islands between 1727 and 1731 indicate that the trade
was also profitably conducted there during those years. The documents
pertain to 112 slaves arriving in 1727, 91 in 1729, 1,306 in 1730, and
1,773 in 1731. These slaves were measured at 2,388 piezas and sold for
759,244 pesos. The calculations shown in Appendix 10 indicate a 36.3
percent rate of profitability on these fifteen cargoes.[6]

TABLE 34. Estimated Profitability of the Slave Trade at Cartagena, Porto Bello and
Panama, and Buenos Aires, 1714–21

Period and Factory	Profitability Rate Percentage			
	Slaves Bought in Africa and Sent Directly to Factory	Slaves Bought in Africa and Refreshed in Islands	Slaves Bought in Islands	Average Profitability
1714–18				
Cartagena	42.7	—	1.6	10.0
1714–19				
Buenos Aires	25.7	—	—	25.7
1714–18, 1721				
Porto Bello and Panama	68.1	66.1	46.1	57.1

SOURCE: See Appendices 4–9.

An estimate prepared in the early 1730s by the agents at Havana allows us to calculate the rate of profitability for slaves sold at that factory. As Table 35 shows, the estimated expenditure per slave, including charges for purchase, transportation, and maintenance (and excluding commission and duty), amounted to 137 pesos. Based on a sale price of 250 pesos, the agents predicted a profit of 38.9 percent. The actual returns for that factory for the period between November 10, 1730, and July 20, 1731, show that the rate of profitability could be a good deal higher than the estimates indicated. The sale of these 906 slaves (771 piezas) realized a profit of 76,458 pesos, or 47.7 percent. Table 36 shows the calculation.

The company's own calculations for the period January 1, 1731, to May 1, 1736, provide a comprehensive picture of the economics of the trade for those years. The accounting is based on 18,250 slaves who were introduced and sold at Porto Bello and Panama, Cartagena, Havana, Santiago de Cuba, Vera Cruz, Buenos Aires, and Caracas. Table 37 shows, by factory, the average expenditure per slave and the proceeds from his or her sale. It reveals the variation between factories regarding the expenditures on the individual slaves and the proceeds from their sale. The table also shows that the company was barely holding its own at Santiago de Cuba, Havana, Vera Cruz, and Buenos Aires.

An even gloomier picture of the health of the trade emerges from a

TABLE 35. Estimates for the Slave Trade to Cuba, c. 1731

Debit	Pesos	Reales
To prime cost of a Negro in Jamaica	120	
To freight of a Negro to Havana	5	
To port charges carrying a Negro to		
Havana	1	
To rent of the Negrory	1	
To Negro keeper		4
To petty charges allowed	1	4
To doctor and medicines	2	
To provisions till sold at ⅔ reales		
per diem		4
To factors' commission at 4%	10	
To King of Spain's duty	33	2⅔
To Judge Conservator's,		
lawyers . . . [salary]	5	2
Total [expenses]	180	

Credit		
Net proceeds of each slave sold in		
Havana for fruits and money	250	
Profit	70	
	[38.9 percent]	

SOURCE: Shelburne MSS, vol. 43, 150–51.

closer examination of the company's financial statement. It reported that the duties incurred by the 18,250 slaves amounted to £122,958, or an average of 30 pesos per slave. When this 30-peso average is added to the purchase price and the other expenditures on the slave, the company appears to have been losing money at all the factories except Porto Bello and Panama, Cartagena, and Caracas (see Table 38). And, as the financial statement also shows, the company was carrying on its books 766,500 pesos (£172,463) in credit extended to buyers of its slaves. Based on previous experience, some of this debt would have proved uncollectable, which would have further reduced the profits. Overall, according to the statement, the expenditures associated with the purchase, sale, and duty payments on the 18,250 slaves amounted to £616,905 3s. 6d. The proceeds from their sale, including outstanding debts, came to £646,500, a profit of 4.8 percent.[7]

TABLE 36. Estimated Returns from Havana, November, 1730–July, 1731

Item	Pesos
Cost, transportation, maintenance, etc. of 906 slaves at 137 pesos each*	124,122
Commission to agents at Havana	10,487
Duty on 771 piezas at 33⅓ pesos per pieza	25,697
Total expenses	160,306
Gross proceeds from sale of slaves	236,765
Profit	76,459
	(47.7 percent)

SOURCE: Calculations based on Shelburne MSS, vol. 43, 150–51; vol. 44, 911; AGI, Indiferente, 2809, 2812, 2815, 2816.
*As estimated by the agents in Table 35.

TABLE 37. South Sea Company's Accounting of Expenditures and Receipts per Slave, 1731–36

Factory	Number of Slaves Delivered	Purchase Price and Expenses per Slave (pesos)	Average Selling Price
Porto Bello and Panama	6,987	124	177
Cartagena	4,022	132	195
Havana	2,353	116	134
Santiago de Cuba	693	115	128
Vera Cruz	678	119	130
Buenos Aires	3,217	86	97
Caracas	300	117	167

SOURCE: Shelburne MSS, vol. 43, 428–29.

This financial report, which was presumably drawn up for the information of the shareholders, raises certain doubts about its overall accuracy. The directors of the South Sea Company were not noted for their honesty, and it may well be that they falsified the figures relating to the proceeds from the sale of the slaves. There is one good reason for believing that this was the case. The average selling price of the slaves (see Table 37) as reported by the company seems too low. All other records, including

TABLE 38. South Sea Company's Expenditures and Receipts per Slave, 1731–36

Factory	Number of Slaves Delivered	Purchase Price, Related Expenses, and Duty (pesos)	Average Selling Price
Porto Bello and Panama	6,987	154	177
Cartagena	4,022	162	195
Havana	2,353	146	134
Santiago de Cuba	693	145	128
Vera Cruz	678	149	130
Buenos Aires	3,217	116	97
Caracas	300	147	167

SOURCE: Calculations based on Shelburne MSS, vol. 43, 428–29.

the company's own estimates (see Appendix 11), show much higher prices than those indicated in the financial statement.

Although the returns from Havana for 1731–32 (see Table 36) cannot by themselves make a convincing case for the profitability of the trade during the 1730s, they certainly help to cast doubt on the company's credibility. Even more serious questions are raised when the company's statement is compared with one submitted by the agents at Buenos Aires for a roughly similar period, October, 1730, to October, 1736. The agents handled 3,875 slaves, with total expenditures of 375,032 pesos. The proceeds from the sale of 3,800 of these slaves (including 1,124 who died) was 534,980 pesos, and the estimated value of the remaining seventy-five (who were not sold) was 6,750 pesos. Thus the total proceeds, including the estimate for the seventy-five on hand, was 541,730 pesos. On the strength of these figures, the agents reported a profit of 166,697 pesos.

These returns, however, made no allowance for the duty on each pieza. The records that deal with the arrival and measurement of the slaves show that 3,652 of them amounted to 2,945 piezas. Assuming that the remaining 223 were measured at the rate of four slaves for every three piezas, there would be 167 piezas. The duty paid on the resulting 3,112 piezas was therefore 103,723 pesos. As Table 39 shows, when the duty is included, the total cost of the slaves is increased to 478,755 pesos. In any case, a profit of 62,975 pesos (13.2 percent) would have been realized. This calculation stands in marked contrast to the company's financial statement, which implies that the trade in Buenos Aires was unprofitable during that period. The discovery of similar data for other factories might serve to cast further doubt on the reliability of the company's own calculations.[8]

Finally, as has been noted, many of the slaves (50 percent or more at the smaller markets) were exchanged for a commodity rather than for cash. Even when cash was received, the agents often used it immediately to purchase commodities. Taking compensation for slaves in the "fruits of the country" seems to have been generally profitable. In 1733 the company's accountant prepared an estimate of the results if 600 slaves were sold at Caracas, the proceeds invested in cocoa, and the cocoa sold either at Vera Cruz or in England (see Appendix 12). The essential conclusions were:

Profit on 600 slaves sold at Caracas   £5,401 (24,004 pesos)
Profit on £5,401 invested in cocoa for resale at
    Vera Cruz   £11,555 (51,356 pesos)

TABLE 39. Returns from Buenos Aires, 1730–36

Debit	Pesos	Reales
To cost, etc., of 223 slaves on hand, October 1730, at 90 pesos each	20,070	
To cost, freight, etc., of 3,652 slaves received between October 1730 and October 1736	306,941	2½
Costs at Buenos Aires	48,021	1½
To duty on 3,112 piezas	103,723	
Total costs	478,755	4

Credit	Pesos	
Proceeds from sale of 3,800 slaves	534,980	
To value of remaining 75 at 90 pesos each	6,750	
Total	541,730	
Profit on trade	62,975	
	(13.2 percent)	

SOURCE: Shelburne MSS, vol. 44, 542; AGI, Indiferente, 2800; de Studer, *La trata de negros*, cuadro V.

Profit on £5,401 invested in cocoa for resale in
  England   £6,990 (31,067 pesos)

Even if the company chose to take a smaller profit by reselling the cocoa in England, it would still realize 29 percent on a capital investment of £24,299 (107,996 pesos).

The profit margin on hides from Buenos Aires must have been substantial also, since the company was eager to import them. Records show that between 1716 and 1719 the company invested at least one-third of its Buenos Aires receipts from slave sales in hides.[9]

This analysis of the records of the South Sea Company, while not definitive in view of the lacunae and the inconsistencies in the extant documents, certainly leads to the conclusion that the company's venture into the slave trade was far from unprofitable. In fact, its profits appear to have been better than good, even allowing for the variations over time and from place to place. True, these profits tended to be more apparent than real, since a good deal of the money owed to the company could not be collected. Yet, unlike the Royal African Company, the South Sea Company never complained that the slave trade was a financial burden too heavy to be borne.

NOTES

1. For discussions of profitability, see Richard Bean and Robert Paul Thomas, "The Fishers of Men: The Profits of the Slave Trade," *Journal of Economic History* 34, no. 4 (Dec., 1974), 885–914; F. E. Hyde, B. B. Parkinson, and S. Marriner, "The Nature and Profitability of the Liverpool Slave Trade," *Economic History Review*, 2d ser., 5 (1952–53), 368–77; Robert Stein, "The Profitability of the Nantes Slave Trade, 1783–1792," *Journal of Economic History* 35, no. 4 (Dec. 1975), 779–93; and David Richardson, "Profits in the Liverpool Slave Trade: The Accounts of William Davenport, 1757–1784," in Anstey and Hair, *Liverpool, the African Slave Trade and Abolition*, pp. 60–90.

2. One of the cost factors in the company's activities which is also most difficult to estimate is the debit due to wartime confiscation of property.

3. Of course, the sum allocated for a particular item was not always used. For example, a slave whose health remained good would not require medical expense; on the other hand, if a slave remained unsold beyond twelve days, the maintenance charges would increase accordingly. See BM, 25577, p. 131; 25552, pp. 61, 30–51; 25553, pp. 19–21.

4. Here we are using the company's working assumption that the number of piezas in a cargo would be roughly equivalent to three-fourths of the actual heads of slaves that arrived.

5. According to the company's records, the expenditures on these 817 slaves, including purchase and duties, amounted to £19,441 and the proceeds from their sale totaled £37,415, making a profit of £17,974. This profit may well be misleading, for the agents made no allowance for their commission (in this case, 5 percent). If we assume that these expenses amounted to 10 percent of the total sale price of the slaves (5 percent in commission and only 5 percent for other expenses because of an unusually quick sale), expenditures would have been increased to £23,183, reducing the profit to £14,232 (38.0 percent). See Shelburne MSS, vol. 44, 137, 138.

6. We have already shown that during the first period of the trade the expenditures associated with buying a slave in the islands and selling him or her at Porto Bello and Panama amounted to about 142 pesos. By 1730 the commission on sales had risen from 4 to 5 percent of the gross; thus the average of 142 pesos per slave must be revised upward by 3 pesos 4 reales, making a total of 145 pesos 4 reales. (This calculation is based on the average selling price of 231 pesos.) We will continue to assume that all other charges were unchanged, even though the average purchase price of a slave in the islands dropped after 1725. In fact, the company reported that the average expenditure (including purchase price) on slaves delivered at Porto Bello and Panama between 1731 and 1736 was only 124 pesos (see Table 37).

7. The company reported receipts of £32,249 from indulto fines. I have not included this sum in my calculation of the profitability rate, since, strictly speaking, the company neither bought nor sold these slaves. See Shelburne MSS, vol. 43, 428–29.

8. As late as 1736 the company was predicting an overall profit of 22.7 percent on the slave trade. For a breakdown of this estimate, see Appendix 11.

9. The proceeds from the sale of slaves delivered at Buenos Aires between 1716 and 1719 was 588,655 pesos (£132,447). Of this amount the company invested 186,915 pesos (£42,056) in 113,990 hides. See AGI, Contaduría 267, ramos 1–6.

CONCLUSION

The historiography of the slave trade has made tremendous advances within recent years. Although the trade was divided into several national branches, modern research has begun to show that there was much similarity in the mortality rates of slaves and crew, diet, sexual composition of the cargoes, and the tonnage of the ships. Yet much more research needs to be done before we can have a broader understanding of the process by which the slaves were acquired and of their experiences during the Atlantic passage.

Future research will probably establish that the Africans exercised a greater degree of control over the timing and supply of the slaves than has been hitherto believed. The African traders, like their European counterparts, were sharp businessmen who acted in their own best interests and were equally affected by the profit motive. In this respect the slave trade resembled any other commercial enterprise. But since the commodity over which the traders haggled was human, the trade also had a special and distinctive character. No trader could escape the stark reality that he was using human beings as items of commerce. The moral issue did not necessarily bother the trader's conscience. To the African trader, the captives were invariably "outsiders," the residents of a rival state, and this allowed him to ignore their claims on his compassion as a fellow man. To the European, the blacks were another category of men, an alien race strange in manners and culture. The buying and selling of such men did not disturb the Christian conscience, at least not immediately. These prevailing attitudes and perceptions help to explain why African elite groups joined hands with white traders to deprive other Africans of their liberty.

The slave trade exacted enormous social costs from Europeans and Africans alike. Although a few sailors were coerced into service on the slavers, by far the majority of white traders and crews were voluntary par-

ticipants in the human traffic. Economic considerations led such men to
brave the hazards of disease and death. On the whole, these were rational
men who deliberately chose to engage in the African trade and presumably
were prepared to accept any adverse consequences of their decision. No
assessment of the social costs of the trade to the white man can afford to
ignore this important fact.

On the other hand, it must be said that the slaves' role in the trade
was one of coercion. Many failed to survive the physical horrors of the
Atlantic passage; others would die shortly after arriving in the Americas.
Psychologically, the survivors had to confront the wrenching problem of
accepting their status as the property of other men in a strange environment. Some would come to terms with their situation, but others would
offer a stoic resistance to defining themselves as chattel. When it is recalled
that the majority of the slaves were teenagers, their experiences appear all
the more tragically poignant. No historical record can ever completely re-
capture their pain and do justice to their story.

Approximately one-fourth of the slaves who landed in the New World
between the sixteenth and the nineteenth centuries traveled under the British flag. This proportion was more than any other nation could boast. In
terms of its duration, the asiento trade constituted a relatively short, albeit
significant, period in Britain's involvement in the commerce in slaves. With
its guaranteed market, better than average slave prices, and potentially
high profits, the asiento held great promise for the lucky recipient. Actually, however, the South Sea Company never profited financially as much
as it could have from that branch of the slave trade. In addition to being
burdened with corrupt and self-seeking employees and officials, the company was never overly efficient in making the slave deliveries as stipulated
in the contract. To make matters worse, it had to endure competition from
the more commercially flexible and aggressive independent traders. In
time, the trade in other commodities consumed a disproportionate share
of the company's energies. The South Sea Company was also the victim of
the profound changes in the organization of the slave trade that had begun
to occur in the eighteenth century. The chartered company was fast becoming a commercial anachronism; the age of the energetic private trader
was at hand.

The difficulties in its conduct notwithstanding, the asiento had a positive impact on the development of the British slave trade. Not only did the
contract allow the South Sea Company to supply the Spaniards with a significant number of slaves annually, but it paved the way for other English-

men, with the connivance of the Spaniards, to engage in a brisk contraband trade. Even after the contract had been terminated by mutual agreement, the British did not completely relinquish their hold on the highly coveted Spanish markets. During the life of the contract the South Sea Company and the interlopers delivered to the Spanish markets probably as much as one-fourth to one-third of the total number of slaves that the British traders brought to the New World. Although the Englishmen were unable to eliminate entirely the competition from Dutch, French, and Portuguese traders, it can be further estimated that four out of every five slaves who landed in Spanish America during the asiento years traveled in a British-owned vessel. Clearly, the asiento engendered a major expansion in England's share of the international slave trade.

In the final analysis, the effect of the asiento contract on Britain's commerce can be measured in terms other than the number of slaves delivered to the Spaniards and the profits that were earned. The asiento made a more durable contribution by aiding England in the establishment and maintenance of her supremacy in the human traffic. Unquestionably the Englishmen's participation in the important Spanish American markets helped them acquire the requisite expertise and develop the commercial infrastructure to respond effectively to the burgeoning demand for slaves in their own colonies in the middle and late years of the eighteenth century. Seen in this light, the asiento was far from being a liability to the recipient; on the contrary, it served the needs of the British rather well.

APPENDICES

Appendix 1
Estimated Expenditures per Slave Purchased in Jamaica or Barbados, 1714–21

Item	Amount Spent (pesos)
Cost of slave in Jamaica or Barbados	107
Maintenance in the islands at 6d. (1 real) per day for 20 days	2
Commission to agent in the island	4
Duty in the islands	4
Freight to Spanish America	5
Maintenance in Spanish America	3
Medical cost in Spanish America	2
Miscellaneous expenses in Spanish America	2
Agent's commission and/or salary in Spanish America	8*
Judge conservator's salary, lawyer's fees, etc.	5
Total	142 (£32)

SOURCE: Calculations based on BM, 25552, pp. 61, 30–51; 25553, pp. 19–21; 25554, pp. 11, 25, 120; Shelburne MSS, vol. 43, 150–51.
*Based on an average selling price of 200 pesos.

My analysis of the selling prices of slaves in Jamaica and Barbados suggests that the company paid 107 pesos (£24) for the "average" slave. A general knowledge of the operation of the trade in the two islands provides the basis for the assumption that the company's agents kept each slave about twenty days before he was sent to Spanish America. After the slave reached his destination in the Americas, he remained an estimated twelve days at the factory, with resulting maintenance expenses of 3 pesos, calculated on the basis of 2 reales per day. The freight charges to Spanish America, including provisions for the voyage and the wages of the crew, varied, but a fair average would be 5 pesos per slave. Commissions or salaries paid the agents in the islands and at the factories were subject to change, but the commission allowed the agents in Jamaica or Barbados was commonly set at 4 percent of the combined overall cost of the slaves and the provisions put on shipboard. The agents in Spanish America who were not paid on a commission basis probably received a salary roughly equivalent to 4 percent of the gross of their business. Using the company's "tariffs" as guides, we can conclude that it cost the company 122 pesos to purchase a slave in the islands and deliver him to Spanish America, and another 20 pesos for expenses related to his sale. No allowance is made in this calculation for slaves who died in transit from the islands to Spanish America. The number of slaves who died during this leg of the journey was statistically negligible.

Appendix 2
Estimated Expenditures on Slaves Purchased in Africa and Sent Directly to Spanish America

In 1734 and again in 1736 the South Sea Company estimated that it would cost 60 pesos to purchase a slave on the African coast and transport him to Buenos Aires. This sum included transportation, wages of crew, provisions, and so on. The average cost of a slave in West Africa during the 1730s was about £6 (27 pesos), calculated on the basis of the prime cost of the commodities exchanged for the slave, so it is clear that the other expenses consumed 33 pesos.

According to the evidence presented in Chapter 2, the South Sea Company paid about £10 (44 pesos) per slave in the early years of the trade. Since charges for provisions and wages remained fairly stable throughout the company's trading years, it may be estimated that the expenditure on a slave brought directly from Africa to Spanish America was 77 pesos. If we include the estimated 20 pesos spent on him at the factory prior to sale, then the total costs amount to 97 pesos (£22).

Based on the findings in Chapter 3, the calculations assume a mortality rate of 15 percent in transit to Spanish America. The company, therefore, did not spend the estimated 77 pesos on each of these dead slaves. I suggest, then, an expenditure of 63 pesos 4 reales on each. It will be recalled (Chapter 1) that in the case of slaves who died during the passage, the company paid only 50 percent of the freight charges. Freight charges on those ships where the company hired the crew, provided the trade goods, the provisions, and so on, averaged about £6 (27 pesos) per slave during the early years of the asiento trade. Using this amount as the standard, I therefore reduced the expenditures on deceased slaves by 13 pesos 4 reales. Freight charges undoubtedly averaged less on those ships owned and operated by private traders (see Chapter 1).

Appendix 3
Estimated Expenditures on Slaves Bought in Africa and "Refreshed" in the Islands

The expenditures on slaves coming from Africa would be increased if the ship called at Jamaica or Barbados to "refresh" its human cargo. There would be some maintenance charges and possibly some medical fees, but no additional freight charges would be exacted, provided that the slaves were shipped to Spanish America on the same ship in which they had arrived from Africa. This was the case in the early years of the asiento trade. One may conjecture that the total expense for each slave in the islands was about 10 pesos (see Table 33), which would cover food, necessary clothing, medical care, supervisors' wages, and perhaps a commission for the agent. Expenses related to maintenance and sale in Spanish America (including duty) would be the same as those for the other slaves, i.e., about 20 pesos per head. Thus the estimated expenditure for a slave in this category would have been 107 pesos.

Appendix 4

Estimated Returns on the Sale of 3,539 Slaves Sent Directly from Africa to Buenos Aires, 1715–19

Item	Expenditures (pesos)	(reales)
Cost, freight, and maintenance of 3,539 slaves— at 97 pesos** each	343,283	
Expenditure on 625 slaves** who died in transit at 63 pesos 4 reales** each	39,687	4
Duty on 2,561 piezas at 33⅓ pesos each	85,358	
Total expenditure on 4,164 slaves**	468,328	4
Receipts from sale of slaves at Buenos Aires	588, 655	
Profit	120,326 (25.7 percent)	5

SOURCE: Calculations based on AGI, Indiferente, 2800; Contaduría 267, ramos 1–6; 268, ramo 7.

*Five hundred died after arrival but before sale; computation assumes full costs.

**Estimated as explained in Appendices 1, 2, and 3.

Appendix 5
Estimated Returns on the Sale of 362 Slaves Sent Directly from Africa to Cartagena, 1714–18

Item	Expenditures (pesos)
Cost and freight of 362 slaves at 77 pesos* each**	27,874
Cost and freight of 64 who died in transit, at 63 pesos 4 reales* each	4,064
Expenditure on 362 slaves at Cartagena	3,974
Agents' commission at 4 percent*	2,845
Duty on 333 piezas at 33⅓ pesos each	11,099
Total expenses	49,856
Receipts from sale of 362 slaves at Cartagena	71,132
Profit	21,276
	(42.7 percent)

SOURCE: Calculations based on AGI, Contaduría 267, ramos 1–6; Indiferente, 2809, 2813; Palacios Preciado, *La Trata de Negros*, p. 266.

*Estimated as explained in Appendices 1, 2, and 3.

**Reduced from 97 pesos because the records show the actual expenditures at the factory.

Appendix 6
Estimated Returns on the Sale of 1,056 Slaves Purchased at Jamaica and Barbados and Sold at Cartagena, 1714–18

Item	Expenditures (pesos)
Cost and freight of 1,056 slaves at 122 pesos* each	128,832
Maintenance costs at Cartagena	22,962
Duty on 966 piezas at 33⅓ pesos each	32,197
Agents' salaries or commission at 4 percent*	7,790
Total expenses	191,781
Receipts from sale of slaves	194,755
Profit	2,974
	(1.6 percent)

SOURCE: Calculations based on AGI, Contaduría 267, ramos 1–6; Indiferente, 2809, 2813; Palacios Preciado, *La Trata de Negros*, p. 266.

*Estimated as discussed in Appendices 1, 2, and 3. Cost and freight charges are reduced to 122 pesos because the records show the actual expenditures at the factory.

Appendix 7
Estimated Returns on the Sale of 1,561 Slaves Purchased at Barbados and Jamaica and Sold at Porto Bello and Panama, 1715–18, 1721

Item	Expenditures (pesos)
Cost, freight, maintenance, etc. of 1,561 slaves at 142 pesos* each	221,662
Duty on 1,104 piezas at 33⅓ pesos each	36,796
Total expenses	258,458
Receipts from sale of slaves	377,595
Profit	119,137
	(46.1 percent)

SOURCE: Calculations based on AGI, Contaduría 267, ramos 1–6; Indiferente, 2810, 2813, 2816.

*Estimated as discussed in Appendices 1, 2, and 3.

Appendix 8
Estimated Returns on the Sale of 435 Slaves Sent Directly from Africa to Porto Bello and Panama, 1715–18, 1721

Item	Expenditures (pesos)
Cost, freight, and maintenance of 435 slaves at 97 pesos* each	42,195
Cost and freight of 77 slaves who died in transit at 63 pesos 4 reales* each	4,890
Duty on 299 piezas at 33⅓ pesos each	9,966
Total expenses	57,051
Receipts from sale of slaves	95,874
Profit	38,823
	(68.1 percent)

SOURCE: Calculations based on AGI, Contaduría 267, ramos 1–6; Indiferente, 2810, 2813, 2816.

* Estimated as discussed in Appendices 1, 2, and 3.

Appendix 9
Estimated Returns on the Sale of 1,753 Slaves Purchased in Africa, Refreshed at Jamaica and Barbados, and Sold at Porto Bello and Panama, 1715–18, 1721

Item	Expenditures (pesos)
Cost, freight, and maintenance of 1,753 slaves at 107 pesos* each	187,571
Cost and freight of 309 slaves who died in transit at 63 pesos 4 reales* each	19,622
Duty on 1,203 piezas at 33⅓ pesos each	40,096
Total expenses	247,289
Receipts from sale of slaves	410,624
Profit	163,335
	(66.1 percent)

SOURCE: Calculations based on AGI, Contaduría 267, ramos 1–6; Indiferente, 2810, 2813, 2816.

* Estimated as discussed in Appendices 1, 2, and 3.

Appendix 10
Estimated Returns from Porto Bello and Panama, 1727–31

Item	Expenditures (pesos)
Cost, transportation, maintenance, etc. of 3,282 slaves at 145 pesos 4 reales* each	477,531
Duty on 2,388 piezas at 33⅓ pesos each	79,592
Total expenses	557,123
Receipts from sale of slaves	759,240
Profit	202,117
	(36.3 percent)

SOURCE: Calculations based on Shelburne MSS, vol. 43, 323–25; AGI, Indiferente, 2810, 2813, 2816.

* Estimated as discussed in Appendices 1, 2, and 3. The average cost per slave is revised upward because the agents' commission increased to 5 percent.

Appendix 11
Estimate for the South Sea Company's Trade to Spanish America, c. 1736

Purchase of Slaves and Related Expenses	Pesos	Reales
Cost at Jamaica of 4,500 slaves at 100 pesos each	450,000	
Maintenance at Jamaica of 4,500 slaves for 30 days at 1 real each per day	16,875	
Duty at Jamaica on 4,500 slaves at 4 pesos each	18,000	
Commission on buying 4,500 slaves at 4 pesos each	18,000	
Freight to various ports at 6 pesos each	27,000	
Cost of 800 slaves from Africa sent to Buenos Aires at 60 pesos each	48,000	
Commission on remittances from Spanish America	19,395	
Spain's duty on 4,000 piezas at 33⅓ pesos each	133,333	2½
Total	730,604	2½

Appendix 11 (continued)

Sale of the Slaves and Related Expenses

Number of Slaves	Market	Price of Slaves	Total Amount of Sale	Number of Factors	Commissions etc. (25%)	Balance (pesos)
1,500	Panama and Porto Bello	250	375,000	3	93,750	281,250
800	Cartagena	220	176,000	2	44,000	132,000
600	Havana	250	150,000	2	37,500	112,500
200	Santiago de Cuba	240	48,000	-	12,000	36,000
300	Trinidad	250	75,000	1	18,750	56,250
500	Caracas	250	125,000	2	31,250	93,750
200	Vera Cruz	220	44,000	1	11,000	33,000
300	Comeagua [Comayagua]	250	75,000	1	18,750	56,250
100	Santo Domingo	250	25,000	-	6,250	18,750
800	Buenos Aires	250	200,000	2	50,000	150,000
Totals						
5,300			1,293,000	14	323,250	969,750

Profit: 239,146 pesos (£53,808) (22.7 percent)

SOURCE: Shelburne MSS, vol. 44, 144.

Appendix 12
South Sea Company's Estimates for the Slave
and Cocoa Trade at Caracas, 1733

Item	Pesos
Cost of 600 blacks delivered at Caracas at 118 pesos each	70,800
Spain's duty at 33⅓ pesos per pieza on 500 piezas	16,666⅔
Tariff charges [includes all expenses]	20,530
Total	107,996⅔
Proceeds from the sale of 600 negroes at 220 pesos each	132,000
[Profit]	[24,003⅓ (£5,401)]
Cocoa Accounts, Vera Cruz	
Cost of 4,565 fanegas of cocoa, being the produce of 600 negroes, at 23 pesos per fanega	104,995
Duties and shipping charges at Caracas with freight and shipping charges at Vera Cruz, computed together at 25 percent	26,248.6
Total charges	131,243.6
Proceeds of sale of cocoa at Vera Cruz at 40 pesos per fanega	182,600
[Profit]	[51,356.2 (£11,555)]
Cocoa Account at London	
Cost [and attendant charges] of 4,565 fanegas of cocoa	131,243.6
Sale in London of 4,565 fanegas at £8 per 100 lbs.	162,311.1 [£36,520]
[Profit]	[31,067.3 (£6,990)]

SOURCE: BM, 25554, pp. 28–29.

SELECTED BIBLIOGRAPHY

Manuscript Sources

The documentation for this study was derived almost entirely from manuscript sources located in the British Museum and the Public Record Office, London, and in the Archivo General de Indias, Seville. I also consulted the Lord Shelburne Papers at the Clements Library of the University of Michigan, Ann Arbor.

The British Museum, *Additional Manuscripts*, vols. 25494–584, contained the minutes of the meetings of the court of directors of the South Sea Company. Some of the company's correspondence may also be found in these volumes, although a good deal of it is missing. The diplomatic aspects of the company's relationship with the Spaniards are found in *Additional Manuscripts*, vols. 32768, 32775–800.

The Public Record Office, *Records of the Treasury* (T70), houses the papers of the Royal African Company. These manuscript sources were indispensable for understanding the organization of the slave trade in Africa and the competition that existed between the various European traders. The *Colonial Office Papers* are also preserved here.

The Archivo General de Indias was important for providing documentation on the quantitative and financial aspects of the trade. Two sections, Contaduría and Indiferente General, were particularly useful.

The Shelburne MSS, vols. 43 and 44, yielded information on the economics of the trade. They included significant information on the South Sea Company's conduct of the trade during the 1730s at the factories in Spanish America.

Published Works and Dissertations

AITON, A. S. "The Asiento Treaty as Reflected in the Papers of Lord Shelburne." *Hispanic American Historical Review* 8, no. 2 (1928), 167–77.
AKINJOGBIN, I. A. *Dahomey and Its Neighbours, 1708–1818*. London: Cambridge University Press, 1967.
ANON. *Some Observations on the Assiento Trade as It Has Been Exercised by the*

South Sea Company . . . by a Person Who Resided Several Years at Jamaica. 2d ed. London, 1728.

ANSTEY, ROGER. *The Atlantic Slave Trade and British Abolition 1760–1810.* Atlantic Highlands, N.J.: Humanities Press, 1975.

———. "The Volume and Profitability of the British Slave Trade, 1761–1807." In Stanley L. Engerman and Eugene D. Genovese, eds., *Race and Slavery in the Western Hemisphere: Quantitative Studies.* Princeton, N.J.: Princeton University Press, 1975. Pp. 3–31.

———, and P. E. H. Hair, eds. *Liverpool, the African Slave Trade and Abolition.* Historic Society of Lancashire and Cheshire, Occasional Series no. 2. Bristol: Western Printing Services, 1976.

ASHBURN, P. M. *The Ranks of Death: A Medical History of the Conquest of America.* New York: Coward-McCann, 1947.

ASTLEY, THOMAS. *A New General Collection of Voyages and Travels.* 4 vols. London, 1745–47.

ATKINS, JOHN. *A Voyage to Guinea, Brazil and the West Indies.* London, 1735.

BARBOT, JOHN. *A Description of the Coasts of North and South Guinea.* London, 1732.

BEAN, RICHARD. "A Note on the Relative Importance of Slaves and Gold in West African Imports." *Journal of African History* 15, no. 3 (1974), 351–56.

———. *The British Trans-Atlantic Slave Trade 1650–1775.* New York: Arno Press, 1975.

———, and R. P. THOMAS. "The Fishers of Men: The Profits of the Slave Trade." *Journal of Economic History* 34, no. 4 (Dec., 1974), 885–914.

BORAH, WOODROW, AND S. F. COOK. *The Aboriginal Population of Central Mexico on the Eve of the Spanish Conquest.* Ibero-Americana No. 45. Berkeley: University of California Press, 1963.

———. *Essays in Population History.* Berkeley: University of California Press, 1971.

BOSMAN, WILLIAM. *A New and Accurate Description of the Coast of Guinea.* 1705. Reprinted, New York: Barnes & Noble, 1967.

BOULLE, PIERRE. "Slave Trade, Commercial Organization and Industrial Growth in Eighteenth Century Nantes." *Revue française d'histoire d'Outre-Mer* 59, no. 214 (1972), 70–112.

BROWN, V. L. "Contraband Trade: A Factor in the Decline of Spain's Empire in America." *Hispanic American Historical Review* 8, no. 2 (1928), 178–89.

———. "The South Sea Company and Contraband Trade." *American Historical Review* 31, no. 4 (1926), 662–78.

CHANDLER, DAVID LEE. "Health and Slavery: A Study of Health Conditions among Negro Slaves in the Viceroyalty of New Granada and Its Associated Slave Trade, 1600–1810." Ph.D. thesis, Tulane University, 1972.

COOPER, FREDERICK. "The Problem of Slavery in African Studies." *Journal of African History* 20, no. 1 (1979), 103–25.

CURTIN, PHILIP D. *The Atlantic Slave Trade: A Census.* Madison: University of Wisconsin Press, 1969.

———. *Economic Change in Precolonial Africa: Senegambia in the Era of the Slave Trade.* Madison: University of Wisconsin Press, 1975.

———. "Epidemiology and the Slave Trade." *Political Science Quarterly* 83, no. 2 (June, 1968), 190–216.

———. *The Image of Africa: British Ideas and Action, 1780–1850.* Madison: University of Wisconsin Press, 1964.

———, ed. *Africa Remembered: Narratives by West Africans from the Era of the Slave Trade.* Madison: University of Wisconsin Press, 1967.

DAAKU, K. Y. *Trade and Politics on the Gold Coast, 1600–1720.* London: Oxford University Press, 1970.

DAVIES, K. G. "The Living and the Dead: White Mortality in West Africa, 1684–1732." In Stanley L. Engerman and Eugene D. Genovese, eds., *Race and Slavery in the Western Hemisphere: Quantitative Studies.* Princeton, N.J.: Princeton University Press, 1975. Pp. 83–98.

———. *The Royal African Company.* 1957. Reprinted, New York: Atheneum Press, 1970.

DOBYNS, HENRY F. "Estimating Aboriginal American Population: An Appraisal of Techniques with a New Hemispheric Estimate." *Current Anthropology* 7, no. 4 (Oct., 1966), 396–416.

DONNAN, ELIZABETH. "The Early Days of the South Sea Company, 1711–1718." *Journal of Economic and Business History* 11, no. 3 (1929–30), 419–50.

———, ed. *Documents Illustrative of the Slave Trade to America.* 4 vols. Washington, D.C.: Carnegie Institution, 1930–35.

DUNN, RICHARD S. *Sugar and Slaves: The Rise of the Planter Class in the English West Indies, 1624–1713.* Chapel Hill: University of North Carolina Press, 1972.

ENGERMAN, STANLEY L. "The Slave Trade and British Capital Formation in the Eighteenth Century: A Comment on the Williams Thesis." *Business History Review* 46, no. 4 (Winter, 1972), 430–43.

———, AND EUGENE D. GENOVESE, EDS. *Race and Slavery in the Western Hemisphere: Quantitative Studies.* Princeton, N.J.: Princeton University Press, 1975.

FAGE, J. D. "Slavery and the Slave Trade in the Context of West African History." *Journal of African History* 10, no. 3 (1969), 393–404.

FEINBERG, H. M. "New Data on European Mortality in West Africa: The Dutch on the Guinea Coast, 1719–1760." *Journal of African History* 15, no. 3 (1974), 357–71.

FYFE, CHRISTOPHER. "The Dynamics of African Dispersal: The Transatlantic Slave Trade." In Martin L. Kilson and Robert I. Rotberg, eds., *The African Diaspora: Interpretive Essays*. Cambridge, Mass.: Harvard University Press, 1976. Pp. 57–74.

FYNN, J. K. *Asante and Its Neighbors, 1700–1807*. Evanston, Ill.: Northwestern University Press, 1971.

GEMERY, HENRY A., AND JAN S. HOGENDORN. "The Atlantic Slave Trade: A Tentative Economic Model." *Journal of African History* 15, no. 2 (1974), 223–46.

———. *The Uncommon Market: Essays in the Economic History of the Atlantic Slave Trade*. New York: Academic Press, 1979.

GRANT, DOUGLAS. *The Fortunate Slave: An Illustration of African Slavery in the Early Eighteenth Century*. London: Oxford University Press, 1968.

GRAY, JOHN M. *History of the Gambia*. 1940. Reprinted, London: Frank Cass & Co., 1966.

GREAT BRITAIN. HOUSE OF COMMONS. SELECT COMMITTEE ON THE SLAVE TRADE. "An Abstract of the Evidence . . ." London, J. Phillips, 1792.

HAIR, P. E. H. "The Enslavement of Koelle's Informants." *Journal of African History* 6, no. 2 (1965), 193–203.

HENIGE, DAVID. "John Kabes of Komenda: An Early African Entrepreneur and State Builder." *Journal of African History* 18, no. 1 (1977), 1–19.

HILDNER, E. G. "The Role of the South Sea Company in the Diplomacy Leading to the War of Jenkins' Ear, 1729–1739." *Hispanic American Historical Review* 18, no. 3 (1938), 322–41.

HOPKINS, ANTHONY G. *An Economic History of West Africa*. New York: Columbia University Press, 1973.

HOUSTOUN, JAMES. *Some New and Accurate Observations, Geographical, Natural and Historical . . . of the Situation, Product and Natural History of the Coast of Guinea*. London, 1725.

HYDE, F. E., B. B. PARKINSON, AND S. MARRINER. "The Nature and Profitability of the Liverpool Slave Trade." *Economic History Review*, 2d ser., 5 (1952–53), 368–77.

INIKORI, J. E. "Measuring the Atlantic Slave Trade: An Assessment of Curtin and Anstey." *Journal of African History* 17, no. 2 (1976), 197–223.

JOHNSON, MARION. "The Atlantic Slave Trade and the Economy of West Africa." In Roger Anstey and P. E. H. Hair, eds., *Liverpool, the African Slave Trade and Abolition*. Historic Society of Lancashire and Cheshire, Occasional Series no. 2. Bristol: Western Printing Services, 1976. Pp. 14–38.

———. "The Cowrie Currencies of West Africa." *Journal of African History* 11, no. 1 (1970), 17–49; no. 3 (1970), 331–53.

———. "The Ounce in Eighteenth Century West African Trade." *Journal of African History* 7, no. 2 (1966), 197–214.

Jones, G. I. "Native and Trade Currencies in Southern Nigeria during the Eighteenth and Nineteenth Centuries." *Africa* 28 (1958), 43–54.

Jordan, Winthrop. *White over Black: American Attitudes toward the Negro, 1550–1812*. Baltimore: Penguin Books, 1969.

Kea, R. A. "Firearms and Warfare on the Gold and Slave Coasts from the Sixteenth to the Nineteenth Centuries." *Journal of African History* 12, no. 2 (1971), 185–213.

Kilson, Marion D. "West African Society and the Atlantic Slave Trade, 1441–1865." In Nathan J. Huggins et al., eds., *Key Issues in the Afro-American Experience*. New York: Harcourt Brace Jovanovich, 1971. I, 39–53.

Kilson, Martin L. and Robert I. Rotberg, eds. *The African Diaspora: Interpretive Essays*. Cambridge, Mass.: Harvard University Press, 1976.

Klein, Herbert S. *The Middle Passage: Comparative Studies in the Atlantic Slave Trade*. Princeton, N.J.: Princeton University Press, 1978.

———, and Stanley L. Engerman. "Slave Mortality on British Ships, 1791–1797." In Roger Anstey and P. E. H. Hair, eds., *Liverpool, the African Slave Trade and Abolition*. Historic Society of Lancashire and Cheshire, Occasional Series no. 2. Bristol: Western Printing Services, 1976. Pp. 113–25.

Klein, Martin A. "The Study of Slavery in Africa." *Journal of African History* 19, no. 4 (1978), 509–609.

Kup, A. P. *A History of Sierra Leone 1400–1787*. London: Cambridge University Press, 1962.

Lambrecht, Frank. "Aspects of Evolution and Ecology of Tsetse Flies and Trypanosomiasis in Pre-Historic African Environment." *Journal of African History* 5, no. 1 (1964), 1–24.

Lawrence, A. W. *Trade Castles and Forts of West Africa*. London: Jonathan Cape, 1963.

McLachlan, Jean. *Trade and Peace with Old Spain, 1667–1750*. 1940. Reprinted, New York: Octagon Books, 1974.

Mannix, Daniel P., and Malcolm Cowley. *Black Cargoes: A History of the Atlantic Slave Trade 1518–1865*. New York: Viking Press, 1962.

Martin, Phyllis M. *The External Trade of the Loango Coast 1576–1870*. London: Oxford University Press, 1972.

Mellafe, Rolando. *La introducción de la esclavitud negra en Chile: Tráfico y rutas*. Santiago: Universidad de Chile, 1959.

Meyer, Jean. *L'Armement nantais dans le deuxième moitié du XVIIIe siècle*. Paris: Ecole Pratique des Hautes Etudes, 1969.

Miers, Suzanne, and Igor Kopytoff, eds. *Slavery in Africa: Historical and Anthropological Perspectives*. Madison: University of Wisconsin Press, 1977.

Miller, Joseph C. "The Slave Trade in Congo and Angola." In Martin L. Kilson and Robert I. Rotberg, eds., *The African Diaspora: Interpretive Essays*.

Cambridge, Mass.: Harvard University Press, 1976. Pp. 75–113.

NELSON, G. H. "Contraband Trade under the Asiento, 1730–1739." *American Historical Review* 51 (1945–46), 55–67.

———. "The Asiento System 1730–39." Ph.D. thesis, University of Michigan, 1933.

NETTELS, CURTIS. "England and the Spanish American Trade 1680–1715." *Journal of Modern History* 3 (Mar., 1931), 1–32.

NEWBURY, COLIN W. *The Western Slave Coast and Its Rulers: European Trade and Administration among the Yoruba and Adja-Speaking Peoples of South-Western Nigeria, Southern Dahomey and Togo.* Oxford: Oxford University Press, 1961.

OSBORNE, F. J. "James Castillo, Asiento Agent." *Jamaica Historical Review* 8 (1971), 9–18.

PALACIOS PRECIADO, JORGE. *La trata de negros por Cartagena de Indias, 1650–1750.* Tunja: Universidad Pedagógica y Tecnológica de Colombia, 1973.

PARES, RICHARD. *War and Trade in the West Indies, 1729–1763.* London: Frank Cass & Co., 1963.

PARK, MUNGO. *Travels in the Interior Districts of Africa.* London, 1799.

PITMAN, F. W. *The Development of the British West Indies 1700–1763.* New Haven, Conn.: Yale University Press, 1917.

POLANYI, KARL. *Dahomey and the Slave Trade: An Analysis of an Archaic Economy.* Seattle: University of Washington Press, 1966.

———. "Sortings and the 'Ounce Trade' in the West African Slave Coast." *Journal of African History* 5, no. 3 (1964), 381–93.

POSTMA, JOHANNES. "The Dimensions of the Dutch Slave Trade from West Africa." *Journal of African History* 13, no. 2 (1972), 237–48.

———. "The Dutch Participation in the African Slave Trade, 1675–1795." Ph.D. thesis, Michigan State University, 1970.

———. "The Dutch Slave Trade: A Quantitative Assessment." *Revue française d'histoire d'Outre-Mer* 62, nos. 226–27 (1975), 232–44.

———. "The Origin of African Slaves: The Dutch Activities on the Guinea Coast, 1675–1795." In Stanley L. Engerman and Eugene D. Genovese, eds., *Race and Slavery in the Western Hemisphere: Quantitative Studies.* Princeton, N.J.: Princeton University Press, 1975. Pp. 33–50.

REINHARD, MARCEL R., ANDRÉ ARMENGAUD, AND JACQUES DUPAQUIER. *Histoire générale de la population mondiale.* 3d ed. Paris: Montchrestien, 1968.

RICHARDSON, DAVID. "Profitability in the Bristol-Liverpool Slave Trade." *Revue française d'histoire d'Outre-Mer* 62, nos. 226–27 (1975), 301–8.

———. "Profits in the Liverpool Slave Trade: The Accounts of William Davenport, 1757–1784." In Roger Anstey and P. E. H. Hair, eds., *Liverpool, the African Slave Trade and Abolition.* Historic Society of Lancashire and Cheshire, Occasional Series no. 2. Bristol: Western Printing Services, 1976. Pp. 60–90.

RODNEY, WALTER. "African Slavery and Other Forms of Social Oppression on the Upper Guinea Coast, in the Context of the Atlantic Slave Trade." *Journal of African History* 7, no. 3 (1966), 431–43.

———. *A History of the Upper Guinea Coast, 1545–1800.* London: Oxford University Press, 1970.

ROUT, LESLIE B. *The African Experience in Spanish America, 1502 to the Present Day.* New York: Cambridge University Press, 1976.

RUDNYANSZKY, LESLIE IMRE. "The Caribbean Slave Trade: Jamaica and Barbados, 1680–1770." Ph.D. thesis, Notre Dame University, 1973.

SÁNCHEZ-ALBORNOZ, NICOLÁS. *The Population of Latin America: A History.* Berkeley: University of California Press, 1974.

SCELLE, GEORGES. "The Slave Trade in the Spanish Colonies of America: The Asiento." *American Journal of International Law* 4 (1910), 612–61.

SMITH, ROBERT. "Peace and Palaver, International Relations in Precolonial Africa." *Journal of African History* 14, no. 4 (1973), 599–621.

SNELGRAVE, WILLIAM. *A New Account of Some Parts of Guinea and the Slave Trade.* London, 1734.

SPERLING, JOHN G. *The South Sea Company: An Historical Essay and Bibliographical Finding List.* Cambridge, Mass.: Harvard University Press, 1962.

STEIN, ROBERT. "The Profitability of the Nantes Slave Trade, 1783–1792." *Journal of Economic History* 35, no. 4 (Dec., 1975), 779–93.

STUDER, ELENA F. S. DE. *La trata de negros en el Río de la Plata durante el siglo XVIII.* Buenos Aires: Departamento Editorial, Universidad de Buenos Aires, 1958.

TENKORANG, S. "British Slave Trading Activities on the Gold and Slave Coasts in the Eighteenth Century." M.A. thesis, University of London, 1964.

VILA VILAR, ENRIQUETA. *Hispano-America y el comercio de esclavos: Los asientos portugueses.* Seville: Escuela de Estudios Hispano-Americanos, 1977.

———. "The Large-Scale Introduction of Africans into Vera Cruz and Cartagena." In Vera Rubin and Arthur Tuden, eds., *Comparative Perspectives on Slavery in New World Plantation Societies. Annals of the New York Academy of Sciences* 292 (1977), 267–80.

VILES, PERRY. "The Slaving Interest in the Atlantic Ports, 1763–1792." *French Historical Studies* 7, no. 4 (1972), 529–43.

WOOD, WILLIAM G. "The Annual Ships of the South Sea Company." Ph.D. thesis, University of Illinois, Urbana, 1939.

ZOOK, GEORGE F. *The Company of Royal Adventurers Trading into Africa.* Lancaster, Pa.: New Era Printing Co., 1919.

INDEX

Note on the Author

COLIN A. PALMER, a native of Jamaica, is professor of history at the University of North Carolina at Chapel Hill and a specialist in the fields of slavery and the slave trade. He is the author of *Slaves of a White God: Blacks in Mexico, 1570–1650* (Harvard University Press, 1976) and contributor to several anthologies dealing with slavery and black life and culture.